A Good Telling
Bringing Worship to Life with Story

Kristin Maier

Skinner House Books
Boston

www.skinnerhouse.org

Printed in the United States

Cover and text design by Suzanne Morgan

print ISBN: 978-1-55896-718-2
eBook ISBN: 978-1-55896-721-2

6 5 4 3 2 1
16 15 14 13

Library of Congress Cataloging-in-Publication Data

Maier, Kristin.
    A good telling : bringing worship to life with story / Kristin Maier.
        pages cm
    Includes bibliographical references.
    ISBN 978-1-55896-718-2 (pbk. : alk. paper) 1. Narrative preaching. 2. Storytelling—Religious aspects—Christianity. 3. Story sermons. 4. Public worship. 5. Unitarian Universalist Association. I. Title.
    BV4235.S76M35 2013
    265'.9—dc23
                        2013019150

"The Sun Goddess of the Heavens" is based on an ancient Japanese folktale about the Sun Goddess Amaterasu Omikami. We gratefully acknowledge permission to reprint an adapted version of the story, as written by Keiko Cauley.

Contents

Stories

Introduction

A congregation sits in pews, focused on a figure standing at the front of the sanctuary. She is spinning a tale about the land of the north. Sounds of shifting bodies and rustling programs fall away. The story begins to envelop the room. For a time, the veil between imagination and the solid world of walls and pews thins. The room is soon filled with villagers instead of congregants. Ancient trees materialize and loom overhead. Darkness moves among them, bringing leaves of yellow, orange, and red.

As the listeners wonder if the sun will ever return to the dark and frigid land, the storyteller gives the signal, and the children and adults take out the keys they have been silently holding. Small hands and large hands hold up jangling circles of metal and begin to shake them. The sounds of millions of needles of ice ring out. The sun, knowing the trees have been weeping in the cold, turns once again toward the land of the north.

When the story is brought to a satisfactory end, the walls of the sanctuary re-emerge for the congregation. The forest floor beneath their feet returns to carpet. Yet the story does not leave them entirely. It echoes in their psyches and whispers through the rest of the worship service. It follows them out to coffee hour and travels home with them and into their day. Some piece that rang true has stayed with them. Some questions they have long held have bubbled to the surface. A fullness in their hearts subtly shifts what they know about themselves and their world.

This is what my listeners tell me they experience when I tell a story in worship. It is what I experience myself when I hear a story well told. The amazing power of the human brain to imagine a story as it is being heard and bring it to life in the psyche can feel magical. Good storytelling in worship transports a whole gathered community to a new place of the imagination and heart.

As a Unitarian Universalist minister, I have had many such experiences telling stories to children and adults as part of worship. To make such an experience possible for a room full of people through storytelling is deeply satisfying. And anyone can achieve it.

After a worship service, I often hear someone say, "I could never tell a story like that." I am quick to disagree. We are all storytellers by nature, and telling a story in a way that moves others or brings delight to a worship service is the ordinary kind of magic anyone can weave. Storytelling, like any art form, is less about natural talent and more about applying oneself. Just about anyone can learn to tell a story well, but it involves work and the willingness to take risks, to pay attention, and to care about the quality of the art.

My own journey to becoming a skilled and aware storyteller took place gradually over decades. By pure happenstance, I found myself in the presence of individuals who incorporated truly great storytelling into their work. They told stories in such a way that every part of their telling was true: their words, timing, inflection, movement, emotional expression. Anything that would have detracted from the story and their style of telling simply was not present.

During my first career, as a social studies teacher, I drew on those examples out of pure necessity. I found that if I could not put whatever subject I was teaching into a compelling narrative, I had no hope of engaging my students. As a young teacher, this strategy of developing my skills as a storyteller was not a conscious choice so much as a desperate act of survival.

Later, when I was a ministerial intern, I found myself in the same position that many ministers and lay leaders find themselves—we needed someone (anyone!) to put together a play or story for an multigenerational holiday service. When I volunteered, I had no idea that I would be embarking on a professional and personal journey of storytelling in worship.

Soon, I found myself drawing on everything I had unconsciously absorbed about storytelling from my teachers and my own experience in a classroom. That first holiday service was an adaptation of Menotti's *Amahl and the Night Visitors*, performed for Christmas Eve. The choir prepared songs from the opera while the adult cast invested themselves deeply in a series of vignettes adapted from the libretto. It was a magical Christmas Eve, one in which my understanding of what was possible in worship shifted significantly.

After that service, no multigenerational service felt complete without storytelling of one sort or another. Over several years, I invested myself more and more deeply in the art of storytelling in worship. I honed my skill in recognizing, choosing, and adapting stories with the power to deepen the experience of worship for children and adults. I paid careful attention to the words I chose, my timing, inflection, movement, and emotional expression. I practiced removing anything that would detract from the story and my telling. I worked with it instinctively, word by word, movement by movement, until my telling was as true as I could render it.

Although I had experienced great storytelling as a listener and could draw from those examples, no one had taught me how to tell a story. In many ways, my development as a storyteller was predominantly a process of feeling my way through the dark. That experience of darkness was an exciting discovery in which, moment by moment, I learned about whatever aspect of story and telling was immediately before me.

Perhaps in some manner, any authentic artistic process has elements of feeling one's way through the dark and learning as one goes. Art cannot be a matter of pure calculated technique. Yet feeling one's way through the dark is not everyone's preferred method of learning.

For those of you who long to bring a story to life but have not done so yet, I offer this book as a lit path to begin your own unique journey. You will find within these pages everything you need to offer stories in worship services or classrooms. For those of you who have already begun your practice of storytelling, this book offers an opportunity to reflect upon your process. In sharing the techniques, knowledge, and processes that I employ, I invite you to see your own techniques, knowledge, and processes in a new light. I sincerely hope that such contemplation brings each of you the sense of renewal of your art form that I enjoyed while writing this book.

How to Use This Book

Whatever your level of experience, this book can help you to develop a deeper awareness of how you tell stories. It can bring to light a number of subtle ways you can more effectively tell stories and engage others with them. Whether you are reading stories from a picture book, including them in a sermon, or practicing more traditional storytelling, this book can help you choose powerful stories and develop the skills to relate them in a more profound way.

Quality storytelling begins with quality stories. This book includes eight stories whose themes and plots are ideally suited for multigenerational worship, and which are not yet published in this form anywhere else. Six are original stories created for telling in worship services. Two are classic tales, one an old Christmas Eve favorite, the other an ancient tale from Japan, both adapted for the contemporary listener's ear and sensibilities. Other stories I have enjoyed telling in worship services are referenced in the resources section at the back of the book, along with collections of stories and picture books well suited for worship.

Chapter 1, "The Role of Story in Worship," offers an exploration of how and why story functions as it does for us as human beings, especially within a worship context. If you find yourself fascinated by story, as I do, you will appreciate the opportunity to learn about the sources of its power in our lives and as a tool for spiritual and faith development across all ages.

Chapter 2, "Choosing Stories for Worship," provides concrete advice about how to choose stories that will both engage your congregation or religious education classroom and reflect your religious values. One section addresses the complexities of telling stories from cultures other than one's own and makes suggestions about how to do so in a respectful way that honors the story's culture of origin. It also offers advice about avoiding story lines that work against your purposes for worship in your context.

Chapter 3, "Techniques for a Good Telling," identifies and teaches the most important and basic techniques for telling stories. The chapter explains concrete methods of engaging and affecting listeners, offers practice exercises to help the teller learn to listen for and employ these techniques, and provides a link to online multimedia demonstrations.

Chapter 4, "The Art of Preparation," breaks down the sometimes daunting task of learning and preparing a specific story. The chapter outlines two main methods of learning and performing stories: learning a story scene by scene and learning a story word for word. It also provides step-by-step instructions for preparing one of the most accessible stories for new tellers, "The Island and the Moon."

Chapter 5, "Listener Participation That Works," offers examples of how to draw listeners into a story through active participation. It gives helpful advice on how to successfully initiate, direct, and contain participation from children and adults. A script is included for a telling of "The Sun Goddess of the Heavens," with direction for listener participation.

Chapter 6, "Storytelling by Groups: Drama in Worship," addresses the unique challenges and opportunities of putting together a production in a congregational setting. It considers how to choose a play, skit, readers' theater, or narrator-based drama in light of the capacities and size of your group. It gives helpful tips for how to pull it off logistically and artistically. It also includes a script for "Life Itself" as a narrator-based play for children and/or adults.

Chapter 7, "Starting a Tradition of Storytelling in Your Congregation," offers tools for cultivating new storytellers in your congregation. The chapter identifies key ways of creating a safe and mutually supportive community of tellers.

The conclusion offers some thoughts on how to experience a practice of storytelling as a personal spiritual journey. So that others may join you on that journey, at the back of the book I have included a guide for leading storytelling workshops in your congregation. You will also find a list of resources starting on page 189 to equip you with stories and picture books particularly well suited for worship.

Entering a story, passing through the fire of preparation, and being fully present during the moment of performance have brought me great joy and have pushed me to think more deeply about myself, humanity, and all that is divine. I hope that this book might encourage others to take their first steps on their own journey, and provide an opportunity for reflection and growth for those who have already begun.

Rustle, Rustle, Rustle

Summer was just beginning. While most children were running wild with the heat and fun and freedom of summer, Michael dreaded it already. Living so far from town, Michael knew he would hardly see another kid until the fall. His parents played with him in the evening, but the days themselves stretched long and lonely.

That morning after he finished his chores, his mother told him, "Go, go out and play!"

Michael went out, but what could he play all alone? He slowly wandered down to the river and sat on a fallen log. A tear formed in his eye. He wiped it away quickly, imagining what the boys at school would say. Instead, he just sat, not playing, not thinking, not feeling anything.

Then, out of the corner of his eye, he saw movement. Rustle, rustle, rustle. Michael froze. Rustle, rustle, rustle. A tiny mouselike creature was poking around in the leaves. It was a shrew. Then he heard it. "Eeep, eeep, eeep. Eeep, eeep, eeep." The shrew turned and for a moment locked eyes with him. "Weep, weep, weep. Weep, weep, weep."

As if upon command, the tears welled up in Michael's eyes. A wet river of loneliness rolled down his cheeks. He hung his head and cried. When he finally looked up, the shrew was gone.

Each day after that, when his mother told him, "Go, go out and play," Michael went straight down to the river. If he sat and waited silently, eventually he would hear rustle, rustle, rustle. Rustle, rustle, rustle. The little creature never stayed long. A sudden movement or the shadow of a crane flying overhead would send it scurrying.

Still, every day that Michael went down to the river, he saw the shrew. That is, until one day. Michael waited . . . and waited . . . and waited, but the shrew never appeared.

At supper that night, Michael sat silently, pushing his peas round and round his plate. "Something wrong, son?" his father asked.

Michael set down his fork. "I've been watching this shrew down by the river. I've seen him every day, but today he never came."

"I saw cranes across the river again," said his mother. "Probably one of them got it."

Michael froze.

"Oh, Michael," said his mother. "I know it seems cruel to us, but it's just nature's way."

Michael didn't say a word.

"Son," said his father gently. "We can only have the cranes' beauty because they feed from nature."

All Michael could say was, "I don't think they're beautiful."

The next day, Michael slowly wandered down to the river. He sat on the log, not playing, not thinking, not feeling anything.

Then, out of the corner of his eye, he saw movement. Michael turned, but there was no shrew. It was a large gray bird—a crane. Michael felt the heat of anger rise in his chest, but before he could do anything, the crane turned and locked eyes with him.

"Karororororo," it cried. "Karororororo."

"Cr-r-r-r-r-y. Cr-r-r-r-r-r-y."

As if upon command, the tears welled up in Michael's eyes. A wet river of loneliness rolled down his cheeks. He hung his head and cried. When he finally looked up, the crane was still there.

They stared at one another a long time, boy and bird, the spell broken only by the "karorororororo" of another crane across the river. The bird looked at Michael a moment longer before turning and stretching its wings. It pushed off and pulled itself into the air. Michael watched it glide over the river, land, and walk awkwardly toward its mate.

Watching those birds together, Michael knew they *were* beautiful. Then, as if for the first time, he noticed everything around him. He heard the water rushing. He saw the river reeds waving. He heard frogs and birds and bugs all around him, and he knew. He was not alone. Life was everywhere.

Then, a ways off, he heard rustle, rustle, rustle. Rustle, rustle, rustle.

—by Kristin Maier

CHAPTER 1

The Role of Story in Worship

For human beings, story is an instinctual way of making meaning. When something happens that we don't understand or can't figure out, we immediately find ourselves saying, "Sit down. Tell me what happened—tell me the story." Story is so instinctual that we are often not aware of the way it predominates our way of communicating and making sense of the world. The story of something that has happened is so experientially based that it seems to simply retell an actual experience. And yet, story is so much more complex.

Narrative, that is, the telling and shaping of story, has enjoyed a newfound status in the past few decades in a host of fields, including psychology, education, law, theology, and counseling. The work of such researchers and thinkers as psychologist Jerome Bruner turns our attention to the ways in which much of our thinking happens in narrative form.[1] As we move through our day, most of us find ourselves using narrative, more than formal logic or scientific, rational thinking. Even when we do hear or read a fact, theory, or formula, we rarely let it stand on its own. We fit it into a narrative. We tell what it means in the larger picture.

Any experience we have includes a wash of details, facts, sense perceptions, motivations, events, and actions. We could not possibly reproduce that volume of phenomena exactly as it occurred. Instead, when we tell a story, we offer a swath of that experience, pre-filtered to present a narrative whole that offers some coherent meaning. When we listen to someone else's narrative account, we engage in our

---

[1] See Jerome Bruner, *Actual Minds, Possible Worlds* (Cambridge: Harvard University Press, 1986). Also Jerome Bruner, "The Narrative Construction of Reality," *Critical Inquiry*, 1991, 18:1, 1–21.

own meaning making; we take that swath of experience as presented and weave it into what we already know in order to make sense of it. As we do, our interpretation of that story becomes part of our own larger picture of reality. We make sense of the story we are being told and allow it to shape the larger meaning that we hold.

During the most difficult times of our lives, when we are experiencing serious illness, loss, or trauma, our ability to tell our own story becomes especially important. Sociologist Arthur Frank has written extensively about the experience of "deep illness."[2] When an experience of illness is so deep that it overshadows our life and identity, we are thrown into a kind of chaos. Frank's work has led him to believe that helping people tell their story is essential to healing. Telling one's story, even a story of chaos, begins the process of forcing those incomprehensible events into a kind of structure of meaning. It names what has happened and thus begins to move us out of the realm of chaos. The stories we have to tell may at times be tragic, but they are never without meaning. With meaning, we can move through and toward things like grief, acceptance, and eventually some ray of hope. Story is an irreplaceable tool in this process.

Storying Our Lives

From a very young age to our oldest years, we are constantly "storying" our lives. Day to day, we live in a narrative about who we are, what we believe our fate to be, our history, our potential, our limitations, and our very purpose in life. We embed our deepest spiritual and human beliefs in that story. To a certain extent, the narrative is one of our own making, although deeply influenced by our families, community, and culture. The work of Michael White and David Epston in the field of family therapy reveals the power that storying has over our lives, for good and bad. Through their development of narrative therapy, White and Epston offer

---

[2] See Arthur W. Frank, *At the Will of the Body: Reflections on Illness* (Boston: Mariner/Houghton Mifflin, 1991). Also see Arthur W. Frank, "Just Listening: Narrative and Deep Illness," *Families, Systems and Health*, 1998, 16: 197–212.

insight into recognizing that inaccurate and hurtful storying can trap us in limiting, damaging roles and patterns. Their work also points to the tremendous power that story has to re-author our lives in more truthful, expansive, and life-giving ways.[3]

Engaging Fiction for Meaning Making

A story need not be about one's own personal experience nor even factually true to be rich ground for meaning making. Fictional stories have the power to transport us into another's experience that, for a moment, we live as our own. People easily enter stories that clearly cannot be true, such as those that deal with magic, talking animals, or other fantastic elements. In *Biographia Literaria*, Samuel Taylor Coleridge writes that entering such a story requires the "willful suspension of disbelief." In order to engage with a story, we agree to accept fanciful or implausible elements that set the stage for a narrative that we can enter and experience.

J. R. R. Tolkien argues that this isn't so much suspending disbelief as establishing a "secondary world," the laws of which one accepts while one is in it. The reader does not give up a sense of what is true but adopts what is true within the world of the story. In effect, we allow an alternate set of truths to exist alongside what we know about our actual life and universe.[4]

Although Tolkien refers specifically to "fairy-stories," to some extent we engage this process any time we live a fictional story. We know that the characters are not real, the events they experience did not happen, and yet we experience them as if they are real. The events are happening, at least to a degree, in the moment we live the story.

Tolkien rightly notes that once something rings false within the accepted expansion of plausibility, the spell is broken. Even though we are willing to accept the terms of unreality in order to enter the story, it must still feel true within that contingent reality. The power of story lies in its ability to allow us to experience

---

[3] See Michael White and David Epston, *Narrative Means to Therapeutic Ends* (New York: Norton, 1990).
[4] See J. R. R. Tolkien, "On Fairy-Stories," in *Tree and Leaf* (New York: HarperCollins, 2012).

that which is deeply symbolic. The symbolic can be quite fanciful but ultimately it must be believable at some core level; that is, it must point back to some truth about actual lived experience. Thus, fiction allows us to try on an experience that is in some way novel, yet in another way deeply familiar. In doing so, we encounter a relatively safe way to engage questions about our real lives, experiences, and cast of characters, most especially ourselves.

Through fiction, we can explore what is both symbolic and deeply emotional—a fertile ground for meaning making and one well suited for worship. Bringing fiction into worship allows a congregation to enter this symbolic world together and engage the questions and truths embedded within. Because story, including fiction, can touch universal emotions and concerns, it can bring forward our ultimate concerns, about our lives, our world, and what we know to be divine.

The fictional story "Rustle, Rustle, Rustle," which precedes this chapter, wrestles with several significant human concerns. Layered within questions about impermanence and our place in the natural world is the human experience of loneliness. I recently told this story to a classroom of twenty first graders. After I prepped them by showing them photos of cranes and shrews, I asked one question: "Have you ever felt lonely?" Every head in the room nodded. The looks on their faces told me that at six and seven years of age, they knew what lonely meant and knew it to be a serious emotion. I have also had adults many decades older tell me that they were deeply moved by this same story. The circumstances of "Rustle, Rustle, Rustle" are fictitious, but the experience of loneliness is something most of us struggle through at various times in our lives.

Telling Across Religious Traditions

The prevalence of story in religious traditions speaks to its power as a gateway into meaning making. We need not read these stories as literally true to find a rich record of how ancient peoples expressed the meaning of their lives and an opportunity for us to do the same today. To this day, stories of the ancient Israelites, Zen koans, parables of Jesus, and other religious narratives provide a way for people to wrestle with important spiritual and theological questions. The stories hold opportunities for engaging what we know about humanity, about God, about the universe, and about our most important purposes in life.

Many of the stories from these traditions have endured long beyond the actual culture, history, and theological teachings they came from. Part of the power of narrative and its ability to endure past its original context lies in the fact that narrative is not didactic in nature. It is experiential and therefore requires readers or listeners to make meaning through their own interpretation of the narrative as a whole. If the story provides a window into a substantial or foundational human experience, then its value as raw material for meaning making will endure even as the meaning that is made varies from one historical perspective to another.

Touching the Whole Person

Many of us come to worship because we are hungry for an experience of wholeness. We hope that through worshipping together, we might feel a deeper connection to God, the sacred, each other, or simply our own true selves. Feeling our selves as more whole and as part of a greater whole can be transformative. We may find that in being more connected to our true selves, we are able to be more true to those we love, to strangers, to friends, and to the earth. We may find ourselves reorienting our lives toward our deepest values, living with more compassion and with a deeper awareness of the sacred.

That is at least what we hope will happen in worship. Such an experience cannot be compelled, only invited. When we take on the task of creating worship for a community, we assume the challenge of more effectively making that invitation. We can do so through the worship elements we offer and how skillfully and genuinely we offer them.

A worship service that works touches us as whole people. We hope that worship will stimulate our minds, touch our hearts, and speak to that part of ourselves that is ineffable and somehow irreducible—that part of ourselves we call spirit. The target of worship isn't just our intellect or our emotions but our whole person.

Story as a medium is well suited to communicating with or touching the whole person. To tell or write a story well is to include a full but carefully selected range of sensory details, events, motivations, and feelings. It is also holistic because, when done well, it creates a vicarious experience in the listeners or readers that they must, to some degree, fill in and then interpret for themselves. Obviously, each person's interpretation is shaped by the story and telling, but a true narrative leaves the meaning up to the hearer.

Narrative is multilayered by its very nature and thus creates an opportunity for meaning making that spans a wide range of ages and perspectives. Comprehension of story begins at a very early age. A good story includes elements that engage adults at one level and children at others. Thus, story has the capacity to unite an assembled multigenerational congregation in reflecting on or wrestling with some important issue or experience. Because listening to a story is a highly interpretive act, stories also fit well in a theologically diverse congregation. When a complex story is shared in worship, a distinctly democratic theological endeavor unfolds. People will make of a story what they will.

A story's use of symbols, imagery, and archetypes can aesthetically and thematically inform an entire worship service. It can be paired with music, poetry, prose, visual arts, and preaching to create an overall engaging and cohesive worship experience. A story can serve as a central text alongside scripture or other readings. Themes, ideas, and questions that a story wrestles with can be echoed in a sermon or reappear in prayer or meditation.

Story is robbed of its power if we predetermine the answers that are derived from it, so we must be careful about the extent to which we use a story to make a particular point. However, that doesn't mean story can't deliberately raise questions about our larger goals of worship and congregational life. Story can invite a congregation to deepen its own sense of mission as a community of faith in our world. It can be an artistic way to explore how we may act in the world through social justice activities, pastoral care, or our relational life as a congregation or community. A story heard in worship can be the springboard for engaging particular themes in religious education classes. With their teachers and fellow classmates, children can explore their experience of the story and the extent to which it relates to their own life experiences. It can be the element that invites them to express meaning through visual art or play.

A multigenerational worship team that I was part of used "Rustle, Rustle, Rustle" to give a cohesive theme and imagery to an Easter service. I told the story early in the service while the children were present. Afterward, the children and their teachers left to prepare a surprise for the congregation. The minister then delivered a sermon that was developmentally appropriate for adults and addressed the Easter narrative and many of the issues raised in the story—life, death, impermanence, and connection. Meanwhile, the adult teachers helped the children process the story through activities developmentally appropriate for them. After the sermon, the children returned with their surprise Easter parade, complete with balloons and giant paper cranes.

Telling or Reading

Stories can be communicated in a variety of ways in a religious context. In many congregations, a religious educator or a minister sits near the front of a sanctuary with a picture book, surrounded by a crowd of children. There are many wonderful children's picture books that address a wide range of themes which can augment a worship service. Even relatively young children can explore religious and ethical issues when they are raised through picture books that offer illustrations and carefully crafted language that is reasonably accessible. Reading a story from a picture book is a relatively low-risk way to offer children a foothold in a worship service that might otherwise mostly exclude them.

There are inherent limitations to reading picture books in worship, however, including scale. The picture book is an art form that depends upon intimacy. It works best when children sit next to the person reading the story. Effective illustrations draw the viewer into details that dynamically shape, and are shaped by, the work as a whole. You have to be close to see them.

Some congregations are small enough to allow the kind of intimate circle that works so well with a picture book. However, even when all of the children who come forward can see the book, the adults are too far away to see. The multigenerational element is lost when the adults get the message that this time is not for them. Sometimes the messages and experiences in the stories are needed as much if not more by the adults. Very small congregations may have the problem of having only a few children in the worship service. Some children are intimidated by being called up to a circle in front of a larger, adult audience, yet staying in the pew makes it difficult or impossible to see the artwork in the book.

Some books are available in giant-sized print versions. The larger-than-life size, in and of itself, can lend an extra sense of magic to the reading. Unfortunately, the selection of oversized books is limited. Projecting the illustrations of a book onto a screen allows all or most of the congregation to share in the visual imagery and is a good option if you have the equipment in your sanctuary. However, using projected images does shift the experience of the book in a significant way. The intimacy of that side-by-side sharing between reader and listener is lost.

In spite of the limitations of reading picture books in a worship service, a good story, read well, can expand the breadth and depth of the worship experience for children and adults. It can bring humor, delight, and gentle pathos to worship. The more skillfully a picture book is read, the more the story will transcend limitations and create a powerful effect in a worship service. Chapter 2 explains how to choose books that are appropriate for a worship service, several examples of which are included in the list of resources at the end of the book. The techniques detailed in Chapter 3 will help you to read those stories in ways that maximize their power.

Storytelling requires more preparation and a little more risk taking than reading from a picture book yet is suited especially well for worship. Its immediacy and intimacy translate well to a worship setting—there is literally nothing between the teller and the listeners. With a picture book, I direct your attention to me to hear the words and then to the book to see the pictures. That isn't necessarily bad, but it means that two elements compete to convey the story. In storytelling, listeners focus on only one point, experiencing more of the story in their imagination, filling it with their own familiar and meaningful images and sense memories. The primary canvas is the listener's imagination.

When the telling of a story evokes all the senses, it actively engages the imagination of the listener. Inviting the listener into a narrative based on lived sensory experience activates many realms of the brain, including language, sight, smell, physical movement, and a sense of time. It also evokes emotions such as dread, anxiety (just enough to make it interesting), relief, and joy. In effect, the listener becomes co-creator. This is true in any art form but especially storytelling. Perhaps because most of us are visually oriented, and storytelling relies predominantly on auditory input, the listener assumes a highly active role of imagining the story.

Storytelling can be effective with any size gathering. With practice, a storyteller can become skilled at playing to every corner of the room, to every age, and to everyone gathered. The storyteller creates a relationship with each listener by speaking to each person in the room. This relationship is different from the one created by a play or a musical, in which the listener is like a fly on the wall. Instead, the leader develops a relationship with you by telling you, personally, a story. It is a community-building experience because of the relationship between teller and listener and because the listeners share a common experience of living a particular story.

A Gift to the Teller

Storytelling in worship can be a lovely experience for a storyteller. We are not busking stories on a street corner; we aren't telling them at a birthday party; we aren't at a coffeehouse. We are engaging in worship—a very specific context. In a worshipping community there is a built-in respect for the power of story. Listeners tend to be respectful and kind even to novice tellers. There is an ethos of accepting each other with all of our vulnerabilities and strengths that allows tellers to risk making mistakes. Because traditional worship services are so often not engaging for children, they tend to be hungry for story and thus a pretty darn good audience. It also helps that children know that they are expected to be on their best behavior and that their parents or grandparents are present and watching.

In addition, there are minimal distractions in a service. The kids tend to be focused on the story. Unlike in a coffee shop or library, people aren't ordering food or drinks, there are no laptops, phones are (supposed to be) in silent mode. A worship service is a much easier storytelling gig in lots of ways than most other venues.

Because the time frame of worship usually allows for only a single story, the teller has the opportunity to focus on that one story fully, to render it in all its depth, nuance, and meaning. People who love stories and love to tell stories know that good storytelling is more than entertainment. It is the transportation of the soul to new territory. People come to church with an openness to deeper meaning and an openness to experiences of awe, reverence, and human pathos. They want the storyteller to succeed in telling a transformative story, because they want to have that experience of transformation. It is a set-up for success for everyone involved.

Storytelling as Art Form

Art involves making expressive and aesthetic choices. It also requires an awareness of how those choices affect how we make meaning. As an act of communication, art is relational in nature. To engage storytelling as an art form, then, is to step forward on a journey of understanding more deeply how your choices affect others when you share a story. This book does offer concrete techniques to enhance and improve your telling of a story. But ultimately, the choice of when, how, and whether to use those techniques is your own.

To be an artist is to be in a growing but always limited state of awareness, both about the truth we speak and how we speak it. If we experience that deeper awareness of technique as devaluing criticism, the opportunity to experience art gets shut off. Although art continually demands that we expand our awareness, there is no perfection in art. If given the power, this unattainable illusion of perfection can prevent us from even starting on this beautiful, rich journey of storytelling.

The beauty of this lack of perfection is that it does not matter where you are on the path. Someone just starting to think about storytelling is engaged as deeply in the art as an experienced teller working on some subtle nuance. Both are reaching to communicate, making choices to do so in aesthetically moving and meaningful ways, and growing in the process.

More than anything, good storytelling is a matter of simply developing the skills you already have as a human being who creates and tells stories every day. If you have any social relationships, if you have ever strung events together in order to tell what has happened, if you have ever told a child a bedtime story or shared a funny story with friends over coffee, you have already been a storyteller. Bringing such storytelling into worship is a relatively small step forward.

Petula and the Brindleberry Flower

In the kingdom of Paeonia, under the rule of good king Helleborus, lay a valley known for its beautiful flowers. In that valley was a village whose market square was bustling, for King Helleborus was coming to visit soon. In fact, on that very day, the Royal Inspector of Visits and Destinations was in the village preparing for the visit.

"Hmmm," said Inspector Crambe, eyeing the colorful stalls. "Everything seems in order." Anything that had not passed Crambe's inspection had been removed. Now, the market was filled with only the finest clothing, the best food, and the most beautiful flowers.

In another corner of the valley, too lowly to be noticed by most, a little girl named Petula lived with her mother and brothers and sisters. Petula's family had few possessions, but they had a delightful garden. Petula loved living things and could play for hours among the earthworms and field mice and flowers of every sort imaginable.

That day, her mother called her away from the garden to sell flowers in the market. Petula headed toward the village, stopping along the road to pick her favorite blue flowers of the brindleberry bush. She wove the blossoms into garlands, placing one in her hair. She hoped to sell enough to buy a loaf of bread to share with her brothers and sisters.

As she entered the market, she noticed a shiny black beetle scurry over the cobblestones. Fascinated, she scooped it up and walked forward.

Thud. Petula smacked into a wall of black robes.

"Who are you?" scowled the man she had walked into.

"I'm Petula. Who are you, sir?"

"I am Inspector Crambe, Royal Inspector of Visits and Destinations." He peered down at her. "Are those weeds in your hair?"

"No, sir, they're the flowers of the brindleberry bush. Penny a garland," she said, holding one out to him.

"Hmmmph," said the inspector. "The stems are too green and ropey, and the blossoms are puny. You should make your garlands from something more suitable. Like those," he said, pointing to the showy pink blossoms in the stall next to them.

"Oh thank you, sir," curtsied the lady tending the stall. "I pride myself on my blossoms. This here is the Bella Bella flower. The king himself called them 'wonderful' when he visited last."

"Hear that?" said the inspector to the girl. "The king himself called them wonderful. Now move along, young lady, and take those weeds with you."

"Hmmm," said the inspector as he watched her go. "Weeds won't do. Weeds won't do at all."

The next day, a proclamation was read in the village square.

"Hear ye. Hear ye. By order of the Royal Inspector of Visits and Destinations, all blossoms except the Bella Bella flower are officially classified as weeds, hereby outlawed, and shall be removed forthwith."

The Royal Division of Weed Removers set to work immediately. All blossoms except the Bella Bella flower were removed from the market, pulled up from gardens, and mowed down in the roadside. Bella Bella flowers were planted in their place until the whole valley was filled with their full pink blossoms.

"Ahhhh," said Crambe, surveying the work. "Now everything is in order."

Everything but one forgotten corner of the valley, too lowly to be noticed by most. Here, no proclamations were read and no royal weed removers ventured. Instead, a little girl played for hours among the earthworms and field mice and flowers of every sort imaginable.

The morning the king was to arrive, Inspector Crambe made one final tour of the market. To his surprise, he found no flowers.

"Excuse me," said Crambe to the woman tidying the empty flower stall. "Where are your flowers?"

"I'm sorry sir, there are no Bella Bella flowers for sale today."

"I see that. Why not?"

"It's the Bella Bella fungus, sir. It's struck the whole valley."

"That won't do," said Crambe. "The king will be here at noon. Put some other flowers out."

"I can't, sir."

"Why not?"

"Because they've been outlawed."

"Outlawed?! What idiot . . . oh," he said.

Inspector Crambe rushed to the village gardens. He ran out to the roadsides, but all he found were pale, wilting petals. The flowers—all of them—were dead. Crambe slumped to the ground. "Oh!" he said. "What have I done?"

Then, Inspector Crambe felt a tap on his shoulder.

"Garland, sir?"

Could it be? Crambe looked up. A little girl stood before him with pale blue flowers in her hair.

"Penny a garland," she said, holding one out to him.

"Oh," said Crambe. "Look at those beautiful green, ropey stems and those lovely, puny blossoms."

"They're only a penny, sir," said Petula.

"Here," said Crambe, pulling coins out of his pockets. "Take all my money. Just tell me, where did you find them?"

"In my garden, sir."

"Take me there," said Crambe. "Take me there now . . . please."

Petula led Inspector Crambe back to that forgotten corner of the valley where no proclamation had been read, no royal weed removers had ventured. As Crambe entered the garden, he caught his breath. The garden was filled with lush, green brindleberry bushes and their delicate blue flowers. And there, under and around the bushes, were flowers of every sort imaginable, including the perfect pink blossoms of the Bella Bella flower.

Crambe stood. "Come, it's not too late."

He grabbed the girl's hand and they rushed toward the village. They arrived just as the king and his royal entourage entered the square.

"Excuse me, excuse me. Coming through! Coming through!" said the inspector as he made his way forward, still holding Petula's hand.

"Your majesty," said Crambe as he bowed low. "May I welcome you to this valley with a small token of its beauty and breadth." Crambe turned to Petula and nodded.

Petula shyly stepped forward, curtsied, and held out a garland of blue flowers. The king looked at the garland. He took it in his hands, placed it on his own head, and said, "Wonderful!"

The next day, a new proclamation was read in the market and in a corner of the valley getting lots of attention under the new royal gardener, Petula's mother.

"Hear ye. Hear ye," the proclamation read. "All flowers are now welcome in the market—flowers with green ropey stems and flowers with thick stalks, flowers with little blue blossoms and flowers with large pink blossoms. Flowers of every sort imaginable have their place in the kingdom of Paeonia, under the rule of the good king Helleborus."

—by Kristin Maier

CHAPTER 2

Choosing Stories for Worship

Without question, the most important step in preparing to tell a story for a worship service is the first one: choosing a good story. No matter how skillfully you tell the story, its ultimate impact will only be as powerful as its raw material. The most exquisite storytelling technique will simply fall flat if the content of the story is not meaningful or engaging enough to satisfy the hearer. And a good story can shine through many of the mistakes we might make in the telling.

Understanding Our Purposes for Worship

Asking ourselves to think about what kind of story is fitting for worship is an opportunity to think more deeply about our very purposes for worship. The word *worship* comes from the Old English *weorthscipe*, or "worth-ship." The roots of the word point toward an understanding of worship as an act of naming and recognizing that which is ultimately worthy, whether we identify that as God, love, compassion, justice, all existence, or the interdependent web of being. By turning ourselves toward that which we know as sacred—or worshipping—we not only name the sacred but also encounter it.

We name and honor what is most worthy in our lives through hymns, stories, sermons, prayers, meditations, and other acts of worship. We honor what we know and understand of God, of the holy, of the sacredness of life. We hold up the virtues we value most: reverence, gratitude, humility, service, love. The stories we share in our worship services need to reflect those virtues and honor what we name as sacred and of ultimate worth.

As you consider the kinds of stories you want to bring into your services, spend some time reflecting upon your goals for worship. What is it that you hope will happen in a worship service? What are the collective hopes of those responsible for creating worship? If worship services are planned by a team or a committee, you will likely reflect upon these questions together. If you have not done this recently, or ever, make some time to do so.

What are the shared beliefs (or the range of beliefs) in your congregation about the character of God or what you understand as most sacred about life? What do you understand to be our main job or role as human beings and how are we called to relate to one another? How is this named/addressed/explored through your worship services? What is saving about your tradition and your gathered religious community? What saving experience does your worship offer to those attending?

Religious traditions and even particular congregations within a tradition vary significantly. I cannot begin to imagine one set of criteria for worship that would be fitting across all settings. Ultimately, it doesn't matter whether your worship fits someone else's prescription. What matters is that you are thoughtful about your own tradition and context. I encourage you to think about these questions and how they affect your understanding of your purposes for worship and thus the stories that you select to further those purposes.

Within my own context of Unitarian Universalism, the extent to which congregations use traditional language such as *God*, *salvation*, or *prayer* varies widely. The foundational questions about what we know and name as sacred, and what we know and name as our highest purposes and intentions, however, remain. Eschewing traditional language does not excuse us from asking these questions, but we do so with different language and, to some degree, from a different perspective.

For congregations that do use traditional theological language, the questions of purpose are not immediately resolved. Rather, the challenge is to define what we mean by these terms. Who is God and what does God offer to us and expect from us? Are there attributes we are clear are *not* of God? How do these answers shape what is and what is not appropriate in worship? The better we understand the common expectations of our worship, and where different expectations are held in tension, the better equipped we are to seek out stories and other elements that appropriately feed and challenge our congregants.

We want our worship services to accurately reflect what we understand to be of the highest worth. We do not, however, want our worship to be purely intellectual. Worship is fundamentally an *experience* of the sacred. Ideally, it touches our minds, bodies, hearts, and spirits. Through worship, we hope to create an experience that moves each person in attendance. As we look for stories that reflect the values of our worship, we also look for stories with the power to touch us on a human and emotional level. We are looking for stories that make our worship deeply affecting and help transform us. We are looking for genuinely "good" stories.

The Elements of Good Stories

To be moving and meaningful in a worship setting or elsewhere, a story must be authentically engaging. The first and perhaps most important measure of whether a story you choose to tell, read, or preach will be engaging to others is that you find it genuinely engaging yourself. Of course, no story is universally appealing, because life experience, personal taste, developmental needs, and other factors vary from person to person. However, your own level of engagement is a good starting place. As you listen to and read stories with an ear toward sharing them, your ability to identify strong, interesting stories will increase. Your understanding of what aspects of a story make it appealing to listeners and readers will deepen. You will find that effective stories do the following.

Include the Unexpected
Some unexpected element must be wrestled with in the context of a story. It doesn't have to be neatly resolved, but it must be present. The unexpected or unusual circumstance can be gentle or startling, funny or serious, common or outlandish. Sometimes the unexpected is described as the conflict or the obstacle of the story. However we name it, a story needs to make us wonder, "What happens next?" A story must introduce to our psyche something that we want to see resolved or

completed. Otherwise, it is not a story; it is simply a description of something we already expect. A mere description with nothing unexpected is as engaging as a grocery list.

Create a Full, Well-Developed Experience
Look for stories that offer a world for the reader or listener to step into. That world can be make-believe but must include enough reality that the listener can enter into a whole experience. A well-developed story will help the reader or listener see, hear, feel, smell, and taste what happens. Stories do not have to be lengthy, but they must tell the story as a person would live it. A degree of verisimilitude is necessary for readers to willingly suspend disbelief and step into another world. When reading a story, reflect on how you get a sense of events happening to actual people, at an actual time (even if fictional or fanciful), and in an actual place.

In most cultures, storytelling was originally passed on as an oral art form. Written versions of folktales sometimes follow this tradition by providing only the skeleton of a story that the teller must flesh out through their own particular telling. Such a story was never intended to be told without the addition of sensations and details that bring it to life. The teller not only had permission to change a folktale, they were expected to do so.

Sometimes in sermons or children's times, I hear accounts that are significantly underdeveloped and am left feeling that there is a whole story still waiting to be told. The preacher or worship leader gives just enough detail to prove a point, but not enough to allow me to enter an experience. I find myself feeling as if I have missed out. If an event is retold merely to prove some point, it probably lacks elements that would make it feel like a real, lived experience.

A story that obviously teaches a point at the expense of being a good, complex, believable story might be better described as an illustration. Illustrations aren't necessarily bad, but sometimes they are a missed opportunity to allow listeners to travel deeper and make their own meaning. If the teller or writer makes the meaning for them, the story won't engage and will likely be boring and, to many readers, even mildly insulting. A full, lifelike story allows all who enter it to make their own meaning.

Speak to the Heart

Look for stories with emotional content. Stories that are intellectually clever but do not touch the heart are simply not engaging or memorable. We come to worship in large part to experience wholeness; stories that merely explore the intellectual will not reach the whole person.

The characters that we come to care about give a story its emotional content. When adults, children, animals, or even anthropomorphized objects are presented fully, we identify with them and care about what happens to them. When these characters wrestle with problems we experience in our own lives, it heightens that emotional content. Stories need not be sad or tragic to have emotional content. Joy, humor, delight, and surprise can be equally transformative.

Engage All Ages Present

When choosing a story for multigenerational audiences, look for those that engage listeners across a wide range of developmental levels. Stories that work for all ages allow the listener to draw some essential truth that is experienced throughout the stages of life. You do not need to target the story solely to the youngest age, however. It should include something to chew on for everyone.

Sometimes, stories in worship are aimed at the youngest audience and become overly cute. There is nothing wrong with sharing a cute story in worship, but if we choose cute over substance, we miss an opportunity. Children have real struggles and concerns, which on a fundamental level are not that different from the struggles and concerns of adults. We all find ourselves at times wrestling with feelings of jealousy, anxiety, loss, fear, and loneliness. Other times we enjoy feelings of pride, joy, excitement, and compassion. We can all engage with stories that have significant themes, even if presented in language and with motifs geared toward children. A teller might also add the occasional reference that adults will enjoy but that will not derail the story for younger listeners. This art form used to be more prevalent in children's programming and can still be done tastefully and skillfully, with a bit of creativity and playfulness.

Finding Sources

Finding a good story on the theme you need for a particular worship service or religious education lesson can be challenging. It helps to cast a wide net and start looking long before the story is needed. Some quality picture books and story collections are included in the list of additional resources beginning on page 189. Don't be shy about asking for a recommendation from a children's librarian or bookseller. Many have read innumerable children's books and may be able to point you to a quality story on a particular theme. Fellow storytellers, teachers, ministers, or religious educators are also good resources for story recommendations.

Picture Books
Illustrated books for children are a wonderful resource for stories to read or tell in worship. They offer engaging, gentle tales that are developmentally appropriate for all ages. Some picture books work best with their illustrations, but many can easily be adapted for telling. Adapting a picture book for telling requires spending some time with the book to become aware of how the story is told with illustrations as much as with language. You will need to bring some of what the illustrations communicate into the telling, either through adding language or through movement, sounds, or other expression. As I work with the retelling of a book, I usually find that some language can drop away because elements can be shown rather than told.

In general, I look for picture book stories that can be told in five to eight minutes. They are usually five hundred to a thousand words in length. Some complex stories may last ten minutes, and anything told with significant participation or performed as a play will take more time. You can tell longer stories, but the story you choose must fit the time available in the service and must be manageable for you as the teller. The best stories are tightly written, without extraneous language. If the story feels overly long as you prepare it or screen it, delete words or lines that do not further the story, or reconsider presenting this particular story.

In general, picture books can be retold in worship services (properly attributed, of course) without violating copyright laws. If the worship services are to be recorded, however, seek the author's permission. Many authors have their own websites with contact information. Emailing a request takes only a moment but shows respect for the author and provides legal protection for you.

Folktales, Myths, and Ancient Stories
There are numerous collections of folktales and myths, many of them online. I have found, however, that some folktales are ill suited for worship. Ancient stories, myths, and folktales were written at a time when little was known about the developmental stages of childhood. Children were viewed as small adults, and there was little awareness that unmitigated exposure to the harshest aspects of life might adversely affect young children.

Folktales from around the world can be a rich resource but they require screening. Often, I've had to look through many before finding one that truly fits my worship context. Alternately, you can reshape a folktale's key elements. Take care to preserve the most important and universal elements while changing or removing those that are distracting or problematic for contemporary listeners. Even so, avoid changing the story so much that the elements that have made it endure are distorted beyond recognition. Also, be wary of taking such liberties that you misrepresent the culture or history from which the story comes.

The folktale "The Sun Goddess of the Heavens," on page 111, comes from Japan's most ancient book, *The Kojiki*. The version included here was inspired by an adaptation created by Keiko Cauley, who developed the youth program for Yoshokai-style aikido. Her adaptation retains many of the most beautiful elements of the story of the Sun Goddess and her brother Susano no Mikoto but is developmentally appropriate for youth aikido students and, fortunately for us, multigenerational worship. The story's underlying themes speak to the importance of making good relationships both through control of the self and through sharing one's gifts with the world.

The story's rich imagery can be woven into sermon, meditation, prayer, and song to resonate theologically. When ancient stories are respectfully reshaped, they are wonderful resources for worship. The adult congregation can explore the less kid-friendly themes of the original stories through the sermon, adult religious education, or other formats.

Sacred Writings

Many wonderful stories are part of the sacred writings of the world religions: Buddhist koans, stories from Hebrew and Christian scripture, Hindu sacred and revered scripture, stories from various Earth-based traditions, and many others. Sharing sacred stories can help children and adults develop respect for other religious traditions. Many stories teach lessons or give insight about human behavior that reach beyond any one tradition. Special care, however, should be taken when sharing stories from sources that are sacred to or revered by others.

When working with texts dear to others' hearts, we must remain true to the spirit of the work and must not take capricious liberties. Storytelling is an oral folk art; we routinely make subtle changes to texts to accommodate the auditory reception of the story. We are expected to sometimes introduce significant changes to the content of the story as well, to make the story our own. A sacred story from outside one's own tradition, however, is not the kind of story to make one's own. It is someone else's story.

Respecting that a sacred story belongs to someone else does not preclude sharing it. We need only think of the hatred and violence that has arisen from interreligious ignorance to know that education and respect for others' stories is absolutely necessary in our world. However, preparing and telling those stories with humility and respect are also absolutely necessary if we are to foster understanding and appreciation rather than perpetuate disrespect and distortion.

Many sacred stories are claimed by multiple religious traditions that understand and interpret them in radically different ways. Reading any story, including a sacred story, is unavoidably an interpretive act. As people with different life experiences, perspectives, and traditions, we will interpret sacred texts differently. For example, a Unitarian Universalist's interpretation of the story of Noah and the great flood will likely differ from an Orthodox Jew's interpretation. Both interpretations will likely differ from that of a Reform Jew or an Evangelical Christian. Some of us will interpret and use this story literally; some will use it as metaphor. Some understand it as the word of God, some as a profoundly valuable but ultimately human story.

Not everyone will be satisfied with how we represent or work with mutually sacred materials. Some will be offended, as we might be by someone else's interpretation. This does not mean, however, that those who disagree should not continue to creatively interpret and adapt sacred material. We need not give someone else license over how we interpret or use stories. But we can respect and acknowledge that the story has a different meaning for someone else. Consider, for example, the Broadway musical *Jesus Christ Superstar*, an artistic interpretation of a sacred narrative that is blasphemous to some and deeply powerful to others.

Storytellers' Collections

There are many collections of stories developed and gathered by storytellers, as well as several manuals on storytelling written by storytellers with a wide range of styles and philosophies of telling stories. Many of them offer specific stories with instructions on how to make them come alive. The list of resources beginning on page 189 includes a number of story collections and manuals. Even if you have not yet ventured into the art of telling stories rather than reading them, these collections may hold gems for you. A truly dynamic, engaging reading is a legitimate way of sharing a story in worship and can work very well for children's time.

Your Own Stories

As you look for stories to share in your worship services, you may discover that you cannot find the story you truly desire. If that is the case, consider writing that story yourself. Write it as you need it to be, with the themes and issues you want it to wrestle with. Continue to rewrite and refine your story so that, step-by-step, it becomes a good, complex story that is fully developed, meaningful, holds something unexpected that we desire to see resolved, and reflects the values we want to explore in worship.

I'll offer one caveat for using your own stories: Leave yourself enough time to both create/write the story and to prepare it for telling. You may find it difficult to adequately prepare a story for telling if the story itself is still in the process of being written. Making artistic choices about how to tell the story while you are still exploring what the story will say can be challenging and time consuming. Telling a story helps me identify many of the small changes I want to make in the text, but the core of the story needs to be resolved before I commit to the telling.

Offering Cross-Cultural Stories

Because human beings are storytelling creatures, every culture on earth has a storytelling tradition. Many stories from these traditions are beautiful, compelling, and timeless. Well told, they give us a glimpse into another time and place, and one more perspective on what it means to be human.

But offering a story from a culture other than one's own can sometimes be a risky business. We worry that we will tell the story wrong and inadvertently insult or hurt someone who identifies with that culture. We worry that our motivations for sharing a story from another culture might be misconstrued. Many of us also worry, though, that by not reaching beyond our own cultural background, we will fail to honor the traditions of all of the children and adults in our pews. By sticking to what feels safe, that is, our own cultural heritage, we inadvertently communicate that stories from other cultures are not important or worthy of being brought into worship.

To some degree, living in a whole, multicultural, loving religious community requires courage. Offering whole, multicultural, loving worship in such a community also requires courage. For there is no formula any of us can follow to safely guarantee that we will not hurt anyone. And, although the desire to stand above critique is human, there is no formula for that either. Whether we are choosing and offering stories, music, ritual, or any aspect of worship, we must do our best to choose respectfully and be sensitive to how our choices affect others. In turn, we can also take responsibility for the effects of these choices and open ourselves to learning along the way.

Complexities of Cross-Cultural Engagement and Worship

The discussion around cross-cultural worship is not new in any of our traditions. Our congregations and our own storytelling will benefit from the hard, courageous work of others if we are willing to inform ourselves about the current thinking on this issue. Many insightful people can help us expand our understanding of loving, respectful cross-cultural engagement.

In particular, we must educate ourselves about cultural misappropriation. This is the borrowing of cultural elements in ways that are disrespectful, dismissive, and even damaging to the culture from which they originated. Cultural and religious practices, arts, and rituals are taken out of context and distorted. Sometimes, the ownership and expertise of the cultural element or practice seem to slip away from the community of origin. Misappropriation often happens when a person or group borrows cultural elements without recognizing how their own culture and community stand in relationship to the original community's history and present struggles. The situation worsens when the pain caused by intentional or unintentional misuse is denied or ignored.

For example, in the United States, many people of European descent have become fascinated with various Native American cultures. This fascination has at times led individuals or groups to develop a sense of expertise or ownership of the practices, art, music, religion, or rituals of these cultures. The people who originally created these practices subtly—or not so subtly—lose the power to define them. This undermining of cultural authority can be considered theft.

A lack of awareness about the larger cultural context—in this case, a long history of past oppression—is part of the problem. Too often, those who are fascinated by the culture are not as interested in the history of oppression and its effects that continue to benefit European Americans and bring suffering to Native peoples and nations. There is a rich tradition of storytelling among many Native American cultures and many beautiful tales. But when we tell stories from these cultures without understanding their contexts, we run the risk of unintentionally perpetuating exploitation or disrespect.

There is a lot to admire about the many Native American cultures in North America. The practices, beliefs, and stories of Native American peoples often emphasize our interconnectedness and have a deeply reverent character that appeals to many European Americans. Our world could benefit greatly from lifting up stories that bring such wisdom, but only if done in a respectful way that does not injure the cultures that created those stories.

Do Your Homework
In order to demonstrate respect for the culture from which a story emerged, first research the cultural and historical context of the story. Learn more about the people from whom the story came. Learn about the richness of their culture, their struggles, and history. Learn about your own culture's relationship to that people and their struggles. Read the story you hope to tell within the context of what you have learned. How does what you have learned affect how you understand and interpret the story? How might this context help you to tell the story more effectively and more truthfully?

Understand Your Motivation
Spend some time examining why you want to tell this particular story. What draws you to this story? What is your goal in telling this story? How do you understand yourself in relationship to the culture and people from whom the story is drawn? What might be lost if you did not tell this story in this context?

Ask Yourself If the Story Is Yours to Tell
As you think about the story in its larger context and your own motivation for telling it, reflect on whether this is a story for you to tell. As storytellers, we often reflect on that question artistically. There are some stories whose tone or style doesn't quite fit our own. It is all the more fitting to reflect on this question in cross-cultural storytelling.

Can you tell this story in a way that honors its origins? How might your telling be received by those present? How might it be received by those not present? Are you in relationship with others better suited to tell this story or to offer another story from their culture? How might you go about developing such a relationship? Consider these questions when deciding if a story is a good fit for you.

Telling a tale from another culture can be a positive, respectful experience that is educational for those outside the culture and affirming for those with roots in that culture. In a particular moment and context, you might be the best (or only) person to share such a story. However, sometimes it is more appropriate to step aside and support others' telling of their own story.

Prepare the Story

The most obvious way to honor any story you tell is to put your best effort into preparing and telling it well. When you respect a story and the culture from which it comes, you'll want to present it in its best light, which requires thoughtful practice and work. Inadequate preparation might leave the impression that you take the story for granted or do not appreciate it as a part of another's culture.

As you prepare, consider interpretations, adaptations, or adjustments you make in light of the story's larger cultural context and the possibility of cultural misappropriation. The very nature of storytelling allows for some degree of variation in the telling. It is an art form that is spoken in relationship to the listeners. When engaging in cross-cultural storytelling, however, extra care must be taken not to distort the story's meaning or connection to its cultural roots.

Develop the characters fully and respectfully through your rehearsal. Take care to present characters brought fully to life rather than caricatures that serve as mere symbols. Take care not to trigger or reinforce the stereotypes and prejudices of the dominant culture.

Think about the mood of the story in relationship to its content and themes. If you are interpreting parts of the story in silly or playful ways, make sure that this interpretation fits with the overall meaning and tone. Make sure that you allow a story its due dignity.

Guide the Congregation's Understanding
Create an introduction to the story that helps your congregation understand the story in context. It doesn't have to be a half-hour treatise that kills the story's aesthetic and mood. But it should name the culture of origin and situate the story in the culture's artistic or religious traditions. Often when I tell a story in worship, I also preach. In the sermon, I speak to the larger story of the community of origin, including the richness of their culture and their resistance to oppressive relationships.

Speak with Humility, Respect, and Sensitivity
To tell a story from another culture is to be a guest within that story. Enter that story with the same consideration you would enter someone else's home. Make sure that the tone you set as the storyteller is one of overt respect and admiration.

Be Open to Feedback and Learning
All any of us can do is our very best to build relationships across cultures with as much respect, sensitivity, and thoughtfulness as we can muster. Even then, we are likely to make mistakes or lack perspective. When we do, the most loving and mature response is not to defend our innocence, but simply to listen, apologize, and learn.

Choosing Themes and Topics Cautiously

I genuinely enjoy many great stories that, upon reflection, simply do not fit my worship context. It isn't that they aren't well crafted—many are well written and engaging. It isn't that they are developmentally inappropriate—although some are. These stories do not fit my worship context because some aspect of them works against the purposes of our worship.

Story is a powerful medium, especially in worship. A story that doesn't fit with your larger purposes can undermine your efforts to build a meaningful worship experience. It is more important that the content of a story affirms the values and purposes of worship than that the story is engaging, creative, or particularly powerful. Most worship leaders can get away with telling a mediocre, bland story that fits with their congregation's spiritual values far more easily than they could tell a thrilling story that contradicts them.

When it comes to the question of what is and isn't appropriate in worship, emotions tend to run high in religious communities. This is partly due to the highly symbolic nature of worship and also because we worship as a group. Everyone has an experience of worship, but no one's experience is exactly the same.

When people care as deeply as they do about the communal sacred space of worship, we need to be especially careful not to introduce unnecessarily disruptive elements. Thankfully, many stories are both engaging and fit with the community's higher ideals. We have plenty of room to simply avoid the stories that are not a good fit for worship and to approach the more challenging stories with care and thoughtfulness.

Most stories we encounter, whether from picture books, folktales, or contemporary collections, were created for a context much broader than worship. Some of the most common themes in these stories can be problematic for worship. Before bringing any story into worship, listen for the following themes. Many of them will work at cross-purposes to religious traditions that emphasize a compassionate and loving God or the belief that we are called to be compassionate and loving toward one another.

Bad Guys versus Good Guys

Often, the main character in a story faces an obstacle represented by an evil or bad person. This is a simple plot device, but it also stands in contrast to the deeper teachings of many religious traditions.

My tradition of Unitarian Universalism originated, in part, from a belief in universal salvation. For centuries, Universalists professed that God is a loving creator who would damn no one to eternal hell. Within contemporary Unitarian Universalism, we profess a belief in the inherent dignity and worth of all people. That doesn't mean people don't do bad things. It doesn't mean that certain individuals cannot be dangerous. It does mean that demonizing others by representing them as evil runs counter to our professed beliefs about the nature of humanity and the sacredness of all creation. When we accept or utilize the easy plot device of introducing a one-dimensional "bad guy," we act contrary to those beliefs.

Some religious traditions profess that we are all children of God. If we accept this premise and the premise that we are not called to judge one another but to leave judgment to God, then to demonize someone, even through fiction, contradicts our religious calling. From the perspective of a loving God capable of saving all, each character ought to have some possibility of redemption. Otherwise, we further the idea that some people are good and others are bad and deserve our judgment. None of us is perfect, and when we perpetuate the good guy/bad guy dichotomy, we force ourselves into an untruth that denies our complexity and capacity for both good and bad. When we do this with our stories for children, we force them to accept the same impossible dichotomy.

When we settle for a plot device that makes one person a one-dimensional villain, we miss an opportunity to tell a good, complex, and essentially truthful story. After all, the best stories read like a Jungian dream analysis, in which we see ourselves or aspects of ourselves in every character. Using dichotomous characters robs us and our listeners of the opportunity to better understand all of who we are.

Uncritical Use of Violence

The presence of violence in stories told in worship presents a myriad of problems. Violence has the potential to undermine the religious values we teach, to be developmentally inappropriate for children, and to re-traumatize those who have suffered the real effects of violence. Some stories that include violence responsibly and directly address the resulting suffering and injustice. As long as they are presented in a sensitive, developmentally appropriate way, such stories can be powerful tools for reflection, teaching, and even personal transformation. However, gratuitously using violence to add excitement to a story, as an easy way to develop the plot, or to attempt to be humorous only fuels our culture's reliance upon violence for entertainment.

The desire to lash out at another person, physically or verbally, is an impulse that most young children cannot yet control. Physically striking another person and mean-spirited teasing, when part of a story's comedy, work against the ethos parents and religious educators are trying to teach. Furthermore, for young children, who have not yet developed a full appreciation of the difference between reality and fantasy, even mildly innocuous violence can be problematic.

Even with the best of intentions, bringing the element of violence into a worship space is risky. Serious thought should be given to how to create a safe container to hold that story and the feelings that arise for people as they experience it. Again, the developmental level of listeners should be taken into consideration. Even if most children go to another part of the church for religious educational programming during the sermon, a few sometimes stay with their parents for the entire service. When preparing a story for adults, I have learned to shape the story for the potential of younger ears being present. Also, when I talk about violence in sermons or stories, I must remember that people who have been victims of violence may be present, and I should shape my words with them in mind. We must develop a respect for the powerful impact of violence, especially in the sacred place we create through worship.

Avoiding gratuitous violence and handling the topic with sensitivity may seem obvious. But violence is so prevalent in our society that we become inured to it and might not notice a seemingly innocuous battle, fight scene, or a bop on the nose in a story. Many ancient stories were written and told in eras in which violence was both common and culturally unchallenged. Some of these stories can be adapted by softening or eliminating the violence. Or they can be told as a way of exploring the impact or origins of violence. Nonetheless, some stories, no matter how redeeming, may be best avoided entirely or left to be told in some other context. Not every story must be shared in our worship services.

Wealth as the End Goal
Many folktales, in particular, tell of impoverished families or individuals whose kindness, hard work, or other virtue leads them to vast, immeasurable wealth. On the surface, these stories feel satisfying—a likeable character is rewarded for doing something good or admirable. Many of these stories portray suffering that comes with poverty or lack of opportunity, and listeners like to see that suffering relieved.

However, these traditional tales usually result in the end of one character or family's suffering without addressing another's.

Another problem is that these tales often portray wealth as the measure of a person's worth. Many of our societal and personal ills result from a profound confusion about the ultimate goal of our lives. In so many ways, we are told that what matters is how many toys we have and how much power and wealth we can accumulate. This message directly contradicts the religious values we teach in our congregations, values that call us to be generous and to care for others. If worship is about naming that which is of highest value, we should avoid telling stories in which wealth is assumed to be the highest good.

Black/White, Bad/Good Imagery

In Western culture, light and dark have long symbolized categorical opposites. White has come to represent all that is good, pure, enlightened, and saintly. Black has come to represent all that is bad, evil, ignorant, and sinister. This white/black, good/bad dichotomy has especially taken root among peoples of European descent, who have benefitted from the oppression of people with darker skin.

Of course, we can take this analysis too far and see something sinister every time the analogy of light and dark is used. Certainly, people of all racial backgrounds and the staunchest allies of racial justice may speak in terms of the dark days of oppression and the light of justice and truth. Even so, portraying all that is evil as dark and all that is good as light is an overused metaphor at best. At worst, it perpetuates a centuries-old justification for oppression.

What an opportunity then, when we find stories that move beyond this tired analogy, to explore the gifts found in the dark. And when we examine stories that do emphasize this analogy of good/bad, black/white, we must weigh its implications as we consider whether to bring this story into worship.

External Beauty as a Measure of Goodness

In stories, how often is the beautiful sister portrayed as the virtuous one? And how often is the ugly, scarred, or mole-ridden sister portrayed as hard-hearted and cruel?

This theme of external beauty as an indicator of value still plays out in popular culture today. When we tell stories with this theme, we send subtle yet pervasive messages to our children about their own value and that of others. We live in a culture that places inordinate pressure on physical appearance. We do not need our stories shared in worship to do that as well.

"Happily Ever After"
Consider the values conveyed by a story that ends, "they lived happily ever after." We all want to experience contentment, joy, and happiness in our lives. Religious communities need to offer a more complex view of human nature and life, however, than happily ever after. Believing that any event in life can be so all-fulfilling that it will result in happily ever after is a set-up for disappointment. Life contains ups and downs, and religious community ideally celebrates with us in times of joy and supports us in times of sorrow. To expect anything other than both joy and sorrow in life is to be unprepared for the long haul.

Happily ever after promotes a view of happiness as a consumer product, rather than the lifelong development of contentment and acceptance of all that is present in life. It also seems to tell us that our story is finished when we find what makes us happy, which simply isn't true. We continue to grow throughout life. Such endings might be charming or entertaining but either ring hollow or are a set-up for what should be life's most joyful events. We should at least consider reshaping these kinds of endings to make our stories more powerful and truthful.

I suggest that we choose stories that do more than rehash a problematic status quo. Many stories can help our congregations wrestle with difficult issues in a direct and healthy way. We simply have to look for them and choose them. Several are suggested in the resources section that begins on page 189.

Stories with themes such as materialism, the good guy/bad guy dichotomy, or even violence could serve as a vehicle for open, meaningful discussion and reflection. Because the imagery of stories can be so powerful, the unpacking process needs to be equally powerful, or the teller is in danger of doing more harm than good. Even as teaching tools, these stories should not be told lightly or capriciously.

We can avoid the stories that are hurtful or reshape them (when appropriate) to make problematic elements less damaging. On the other hand, we need not settle for mediocre or bland stories in their stead. Truly good stories that reach beyond these themes can be found all around us. We can discover them in the rich traditions across the globe, and then share them respectfully and sensitively. We can conjure them from own experiences and imagination. We can listen to stories with an ear for the elements that will transport listeners and the content that will move them, collecting those that are appropriate and powerful for worship.

The Keeper of the Rain

Not so very long ago, in a place not so very different from this one, lived the Keeper of the Rain. Each day, the Keeper of the Rain carefully watched the creatures and plants. When they began to droop with thirst, she whispered the word that brings the rain, and they stood tall again.

Each day, the Keeper of the Rain carefully listened to the rivers and streams. When they swelled to a roar, she whispered the word that sends the rain away, and the waters were quiet again.

After many such days, more than you or I could count, the Keeper of the Rain was weary. She was tired of always watching, always listening, always paying attention to other things and beings.

A new Keeper of the Rain had been born, but he was still a boy. It would be years before he was ready to take over. "I can't wait years," she said. She went to find the boy.

She heard splashing coming from the pond. She peered through the cattails and saw him standing knee-deep in the water. The boy bent over and plunged his hands to the bottom of the pond. He stood up with an armload of muck and a wriggling crayfish.

"He is young," thought the Keeper, "but then again, so was I."

She walked through the cattails and into the water. She bent down and for a few minutes whispered in the boy's ear. When she was done, she stood up, smiled for the first time in ages, and walked away.

The boy watched her for a few minutes, until the crayfish wriggled loose and plopped into the pond. He bent in search of the creature and forgot all about the Keeper and what she had told him.

The boy splashed and played in the water until his lips turned blue and quivered. Then he tromped up through the sand and grass to his favorite sun-warmed rock. It was low and flat and as ancient as the rain. He lay basking in the sun, listening to the peeping frogs, and telling the rock his stories of muck and cattails and crayfish. The rock listened and laughed in that low-rumbling way of rocks.

The next day, the boy splashed and played in the water until his lips turned blue and quivered. Then he tromped up through the sand and grass to the sun-warmed rock. The boy lay basking in the sun, listening to the peeping frogs, telling his stories. Then, all of a sudden, the sky grew dark. The air became cool. A cold wet raindrop fell on his back.

"I don't like rain," said the boy, as more cold raindrops fell. Then, he remembered the Keeper and what she had told him. He spoke the word that sends the rain away. The raindrops stopped. The sun reappeared. The boy lay back down on the rock.

Each day after that, the boy played and splashed in the pond until his lips turned blue and quivered. Then he tromped up through the sand and grass to the sun-warmed rock. He lay basking in the sun, listening to the peeping frogs, and telling his stories. If raindrops came, he simply whispered them away.

Many such days passed. As the boy lay basking in the sun, the rock asked, "Have you noticed, the trees and plants are turning yellow?"

The boy sat up and looked.

"I like the color yellow," said the boy.

"They need rain," said the rock.

"I don't like rain," said the boy.

"I know," said the rock.

Many more such days passed. As the boy lay basking in the sun, the rock asked, "Have you noticed, the trees and plants are turning brown?"

The boy sat up and looked.

"I like the color brown," said the boy.

"They need rain," said the rock.

"I don't like rain," said the boy.

"I know," said the rock.

Many more such days passed, and as the boy lay basking in the sun, the rock asked, "Have you noticed, you have to walk farther to get to your pond?"

The boy sat up and looked.

"Who moved my pond?" asked the boy.

"No one," said the rock. "The pond is shrinking. It needs rain."

The boy sat and listened.

"It's too quiet," said the boy. "The frogs aren't peeping."

"Frogs cannot live without rain," said the rock. "Nothing can."

The boy felt a heaviness in his chest. He had no words to whisper it away. He felt the warm sun on his back that felt so good, and the weight in his chest that felt awful.

Finally, he whispered the word that brings the rain. Cold wet drops fell on his back, but the boy let the rain fall and fall and fall. And when he heard the rivers and streams swell to a roar, he whispered the word that sends the rain away.

"I still don't like rain," said the boy, "but I love my pond."

"I know," said the rock. "I know."

—by Kristin Maier

CHAPTER 3

Techniques for a Good Telling

When a skilled storyteller weaves a tale, we find ourselves quickly pulled into a place in our own imagination. For a short while, we live within the story with minimal awareness of the real world around us or sometimes even of the storyteller. When the story ends, and we become aware of having been transported, we may feel as if the teller worked some magic or possesses some rare talent. In reality, the storyteller employed a number of fairly concrete techniques that helped listeners to enter the story easily and fully. These techniques come so naturally to some of us that we may be largely unconscious of how and when we use them.

As we become more conscious of good storytelling techniques, we expand our ability to make intentional, artistic choices to enhance our telling and the experience of our listeners. This chapter explores several of the most basic techniques for effective storytelling. Learning to use them will enhance the listening experience, whether the story is being told, read, or shared in a sermon. Also included here is a method for practicing each technique. Using the exercises with a partner or working with a video recorder or voice recorder will help you develop a greater awareness of how and when to employ the techniques. Video demonstrations of some of these techniques are available online at www.kristinmaier.com.

Using Your Voice

The foundation for any good storytelling is the quality of the teller's voice. Anyone who has been unable to clearly hear what a storyteller or public speaker is saying knows the importance of a good voice level. It's not necessary to sound like a radio announcer, however. The human voice is as unique as a fingerprint. In telling a story, you want to make the most of your instrument, not someone else's. You want to naturally and authentically use the power of *your own* voice.

A good way to conceptualize making the most of your natural voice is to think of meeting the listener halfway. A voice that is too timid, soft, or breathy makes the listener strain to hear and creates a rift of awareness between the listener and the story. Such a voice fails to open the door widely enough for the listener to enter the world of the story and the story can seem lifeless.

An overreaching voice is too loud, strained, or overly animated for the story. A voice that is too loud gives listeners the impression that they are being shouted at. This is usually distracting and can make listeners leery of entering the story. An overly loud voice may also overwhelm delicate lines or phrases in the story. Perhaps most important, it does not allow for a dynamic telling. If your baseline volume and intensity are one hundred percent, you have nowhere to go in those moments of the story that call for an increase in intensity. You end up with a very flat, if very loud, story. Your voice should be loud enough to be heard while still leaving room to grow louder or softer to fit with the story's dynamics.

A naturally powerful voice is like a good singing voice. The sound starts in the voice box but also resonates in the chest cavity and the head. The teller uses all of the body—chest, throat, and head—as the instrument. Enough energy and air are used to completely fill the body but not to the point of shouting or trying to exceed the teller's range.

Of course, we might easily recognize a lifeless or overreaching voice when listening to someone else, but it can be difficult to recognize those qualities in ourselves. Learning to listen to oneself as if listening to someone else is the key to improving your skills as a teller or reader. Like an artist who develops an eye for seeing line, color, and value, you can develop your ear for hearing how your voice communicates a story. Use a voice or video recorder to listen to your own voice objectively. Or a trusted friend can give you insight that you might not pick up yourself. But more than any technological device or trusted advice, learning to listen to yourself tell a story from the listener's perspective is the most important technique for deepening your understanding of effective storytelling.

Practice

Finding Your Naturally Powerful Voice

Read aloud the first paragraph of the story "The Keeper of the Rain." Use a quiet, empty room where you can give full attention to hearing yourself read.

Begin reading with what feels like your natural speaking voice. Try to be aware of how that sounds to you as a listener.

> *Not so very long ago, in a place not so very different from this one, lived the Keeper of the Rain. Each day, the Keeper of the Rain carefully watched the creatures and plants. When they began to droop with thirst, she whispered the word that brings the rain, and they stood tall again.*

Try reading it with half the volume. How does that change your experience of the story as a listener? How does that change your comfort level as a speaker?

Increase your voice level to roughly twice your natural level. How does that change your experience of the story as a listener? How does that change your comfort level as a speaker?

Is there a level at which you feel more comfortable or familiar as a speaker? Is this the same or different as what felt best as a listener?

Try this same experiment with a voice or video recorder. What did you notice when you were able to give your full attention to listening? Were there any words that were hard to hear? Did the intensity of your volume fit the content, emotion, and action of the story? How did your voice level affect how engaged you were as a listener?

The range of a naturally powerful voice can be loud or soft. Even a whisper can be fully embodied and projected to each person gathered. You can increase the volume and intensity of your voice to emphasize the action or intensity of the story while controlling it enough to avoid overreaching and shouting at your listeners. If the baseline volume and intensity begin in the middle range, you will leave room for a dynamic malleability of your voice in relationship to the dynamics of the story.

Using a microphone expands the dynamic range of your voice. People uncomfortable with using microphones may insist, "I can project." Most people begin projecting to the whole room and then quickly return to their usual speaking volume as their awareness shifts to what they are saying rather than how loudly they are saying it. Some people can project to a whole room and retain some dynamic range to their voice, but they are rare. Even people who can project will benefit

---

Practice

Extending the Dynamic Range of Your Voice

Experiment with increasing the intensity of your voice with the intensity of the story. Listen for the point at which the intensity of your voice may overreach the story itself. Listen for times when a lack of power in your voice creates a disconnect with what is happening in the story. With experimentation, you can find the sweet spot of volume and intensity for each key moment in the story.

Read the following section of "The Keeper of the Rain" aloud. When the typeface increases in size, try subtly increasing the volume of your voice. When the typeface decreases in size, decrease the volume of your voice. Listen for a level of change that fits with the dynamics of the story. Listen for the boundaries of too soft and too loud.

"Each day, the Keeper of the Rain carefully listened to the rivers and streams. When they swelled to a roar, *she whispered the word that sends the rain away, and the waters were quiet again.*

from using a microphone because it allows for a more nuanced telling of a story. It simply enables more subtle shifts in volume. Also, using a microphone provides accessibility to a sizeable population of congregants who have difficulty hearing.

The need to use your voice well is just as important when reading a story. In a worship service, most people will probably not a have good view of the book's illustrations. Unless you are reading to one child on your lap, most of the children around you will at times have a limited view of the illustrations. Your voice needs to be the consistent vehicle for the story. If your voice can carry the story into each listener's imagination, you will engage the whole congregation in a shared experience during the worship service.

The same is true of preachers who are using story in their sermons. How they communicate their story is as important as the choice of story. Good preaching often inspires contemplation and reflection in the listener that sometimes takes the listener away from the sermon but into rich internal territory. The truth is, however, that preachers are also competing with a room full of less reflective voices popping into people's heads—voices talking about financial worries, errands to run, children to tend to, the game that afternoon. As preachers, we need to be more compelling than those voices. Our listeners want our message to be more compelling than their day-to-day worries. If we don't learn to skillfully use our voices when we relate a story—or speak at all in worship—we risk deflating the experience of worship for the congregation.

Using Tempo

Tempo has as much impact on how we experience a story as on how we experience music. Tempo is the rate at which a story moves forward. A story's tempo should vary to some degree based on the story's mood. Yet any storytelling depends on the fundamental process of the listeners hearing and absorbing each individual word or action and using them to build the overall arc of the story. That is to say, they are fitting each brick of the narrative into its place in a larger structure. Ideally, each piece of the narrative is offered to them just as their mind has comprehended where

51

the next piece goes. There is a sense of eager anticipation as they build the story with you.

Dragging Pace

If you hold back too much before giving the next piece of the story, listeners may experience impatience. They may have too much time to think ahead and thus experience the story as predictable or boring. A disconnect develops between the expected tempo and what they actually experience, which can pull them out of the world of the story and into a distracting and possibly annoying awareness of the telling.

A dragging pace can also affect the emotional tone of the story. A slow pace tends to add an air of seriousness. If a slow tempo is mismatched with the emotional tenor of the story, the story may seem overly somber or lifeless.

Frantic Pace

If the pieces are given too quickly, faster than the reader can comprehend or digest, then the story becomes chaotic. The listener doesn't have time to put the each brick of the story into place in the larger narrative. The structure becomes jumbled and the listener misses key plot points. The experience of confusion pulls them out of the world of the story.

While you may intentionally choose to rush action-oriented scenes, an unrelenting feeling of being hurried usually does not allow the listener enough time to experience the emotions of the story and its emotional tenor is lost. Often, the only emotion communicated through a story that feels rushed is the anxiety of the teller.

Flowing Pace

A good base tempo allows enough space between the words for listeners to distinctly hear each word, comprehend it, and connect it to the rest of the story. It moves quickly enough so that listeners feel as if they are experiencing the events as they happen versus waiting for each moment and action to take place. Although each listener invariably digests a story at his or her own rate, look for a pace that generally fits the pace of your audience and the speed of their imagination. Also, a good flowing pace typically leaves room to slow down and speed up with the dynamics of the story.

Practice

Establishing a Good Base Tempo

Read aloud the first two paragraphs of "The Keeper of the Rain," this time listening for a tempo that feels instinctively right for you as a listener. Using a voice recorder or working with a partner who can give you feedback can help you hear yourself more objectively.

> *Not so very long ago, in a place not so very different from this one, lived the Keeper of the Rain. Each day, the Keeper of the Rain carefully watched the creatures and plants. When they began to droop with thirst, she whispered the word that brings the rain, and they stood tall again.*

> *Each day, the Keeper of the Rain carefully listened to the rivers and streams. When they swelled to a roar, she whispered the word that sends the rain away, and the waters were quiet again.*

Try intentionally reading at a pace that is too fast. Then try reading at a pace that is too slow. Read through it one last time at what feels like the ideal tempo for a listener.

What was the experience like as a listener when the tempo was too fast, too slow, or just right? What was your experience as a teller? If you were working with a partner, was your sense of "just right" the same as your partner's? If working with a voice recorder, was your experience listening to yourself different from your experience of reading? What insight did you gain about your own telling and reading?

Elastic Tempo

Once a good base tempo is established, a story can be brought to life by bringing a certain elasticity to your tempo. A metronome may appeal to robots, but as people we experience time as variable—time flies when we are having fun and a hard day drags on. Our storytelling should offer that same elastic experience of time.

For action-oriented moments in the story, move at a pace that allows listeners to fall into the action. If you want them swept up, you need to sweep them along. Just as when driving a car, you accelerate by getting gradually faster as the action or excitement intensifies. Acceleration may be sudden or gradual, depending on the effect you want your listeners to experience. Most stories I tell require a gradual acceleration of tempo. Often, I find that at the end of an action scene, I want to decelerate my audience back to the original tempo or into the next tempo. Some sudden shifts in tempo may intentionally feel like peeling out with tires screeching. Occasionally, the action of the story gives the listeners the experience of stopping on a dime. The tempo should fit naturally with the story so it doesn't distract listeners but instead draws them deeper into the lived experience of the narrative.

Slowing the tempo is just as important as speeding up. Slowing down during emotionally significant portions of the story adds emphasis and helps listeners absorb the emotional elements. These shifts should be subtle enough that listeners experience the effect of the tempo change without being consciously aware of it.

Adjusting the Tempo for Repetition

The use of repetition in a story usually calls for a change in tempo. If the core emotional moment of the story is the repeating line, then often these words are slowed, to emphasize and draw attention to the emotional importance. The moment is stretched slightly to give the listener time to experience and absorb the emotional content of the moment.

If the repetition is a moment of action or a string of events with less emotional gravitas, the tempo usually increases each time the series is repeated. The base tempo is used the first time because listeners hear this information for the first time

Practice

Using an Elastic Tempo

The following are some examples of places in "The Keeper of the Rain" where I stretch or expand the tempo of the story. With a partner or a recording device, read the excerpts from the story below. Follow the tempo instructions in brackets, trying to be aware of the impact of the tempo changes on you as listener.

After many [slightly stretch "many"] *such days, more than you or I could count, the Keeper of the Rain was weary.* [try reading the next line more quickly but with each "always" stretched out] *She was tired of always watching, always listening, always paying attention to other things and beings.*

A new Keeper of the Rain had been born, [short pause] *but he was still a boy. It would be years* [stretch the word "years"] *before he was ready to take over. "I can't wait years," she said.* [read the next line deliberately and slightly slower to communicate the gravity of what she has decided to do] *She went to find the boy.*

She heard splashing coming from the pond. She peered [slightly stretch the word "peered" to give a sense of looking for something] *through the cattails and saw him standing knee-deep in the water. The boy bent over and plunged* [speed up "plunged" because it is a decisive action] *his hands to the bottom of the pond. He stood up with an armload of muck and a wriggling crayfish.*

"He is young," thought the Keeper, "but then again, [short pause] *so was I."*

She walked through the cattails and into the water. [slightly faster reading with her decisive movement through the cattails] *She bent down and for a few minutes* [stretch the "for a few minutes" to give a sense of time] *whispered in the boy's ear. When she was done, she stood up,* [slight pause] *smiled for the first time in ages,* [pause] *and walked away.* [slow to a deliberate pace for "walked away" to emphasize the importance of her leaving the boy with her responsibility]

To better understand the impact of tempo on you as a listener, try reading the story to your partner with no tempo changes. Then try to deliberately stretch or compact the tempo too much. Finally, try to make the tempo changes feel just right for the story. Reflect on how no tempo change or too much tempo change affects you as a listener and a teller. How do you know when you hit the sweet spot of an elastic tempo?

and need to absorb each piece and make sense of it. The second time you tell this series of events, speed it up a bit, because listeners have already heard these events and will recognize them quickly. The third or fourth time this series of events is told, listeners will be able to take the entire chunk of the story and immediately put it into context. Therefore, you should repeat the events more quickly.

Practice

Adjusting the Tempo for Repetition

Read the following sections of "The Keeper of the Rain" aloud. Read the first paragraph at your base tempo. When the series of actions is repeated (in italics), increase the tempo slightly. Return to your base tempo for the lines that are new (not italicized). When the series of actions is repeated again (in italics), increase the tempo even more, returning to your base tempo for the final sentence.

The boy splashed and played in the water until his lips turned blue and quivered. Then he tromped up through the sand and grass to his favorite sun-warmed rock. It was low and flat and as ancient as the rain. He lay basking in the sun, listening to the peeping frogs, and telling the rock his stories of muck and cattails and crayfish. The rock listened and laughed in that low-rumbling way of rocks.

The next day, the boy splashed and played in the water until his lips turned blue and quivered. Then he tromped up through the sand and grass to the sun-warmed rock. The boy lay basking in the sun, listening to the peeping frogs, telling his stories. Then, all of a sudden, the sky grew dark. The air became cool. A cold wet raindrop fell on his back.

"I don't like rain," said the boy, as more cold raindrops fell. Then, he remembered the Keeper and what she had told him. He spoke the word that sends the rain away. The raindrops stopped. The sun reappeared. The boy lay back down on the rock.

Each day after that, the boy played and splashed in the pond until his lips turned blue and quivered. Then he tromped up through the sand and grass to the sun-warmed rock. He lay basking in the sun, listening to the peeping frogs, and telling his stories. If raindrops came, he simply whispered them away.

Establishing and Departing from Rhythm

Read aloud the first two sections below until you are able to deliver them in a consistent way. Make your tempo, tempo changes, and style of delivery parallel.

Many such days passed. As the boy lay basking in the sun, the rock asked, "Have you noticed, the trees and plants are turning yellow?"
The boy sat up and looked.
"I like the color yellow," said the boy.
"They need rain," said the rock.
"I don't like rain," said the boy.
"I know," said the rock.

Many more such days passed. As the boy lay basking in the sun, the rock asked, "Have you noticed, the trees and plants are turning brown?"
The boy sat up and looked.
"I like the color brown," said the boy.
"They need rain," said the rock.
"I don't like rain," said the boy.
"I know," said the rock.

In the next section, experiment with deviating from the rhythm you just established. Try speaking the rock's question a little more slowly and deliberately, creating subtle anticipation of a new question. Try speaking the line "the boy sat up and looked" more quickly and with a sense of urgency and concern.

Many more such days passed, and as the boy lay basking in the sun, the rock asked, "Have you noticed, you have to walk farther to get to your pond?"
The boy sat up and looked.
"Who moved my pond?" asked the boy.

Establishing and Departing from Rhythm

As you continue to work with your story, listen for the places where a natural rhythm may begin to emerge. Patterns of tempo changes, recurring words or phrases, the repetition of a particular style of delivery, or the anticipated shift from one style to another can establish a sense of rhythm. Much like music, the patterns formed in the telling of a story give it texture and a familiarity that helps the listener follow the story and stay engaged.

Once a pattern of telling is established, changing that pattern signals to the listener that something different or important is unfolding. The listener experiences the change in the story in a sensory way as well as through the content itself. With whatever story you are telling, look for opportunities to establish such patterns and then depart from them to increase the dramatic impact.

The Dramatic Pause

As every musician knows, rest notes are as important as the notes that are actually played in music. Similarly, the use of the dramatic pause is an essential technique for good rhythm when storytelling. If not overused or held too long, a pause creates a subtle sense of suspense, which listeners experience without being aware of it. A short phrase in a story is often used to tell listeners that something important is about to happen. It is usually as simple as "suddenly," or "to his surprise," or "without warning." Following this kind of phrase, I pause briefly to let listeners wonder and become curious about what is going to happen. I find it helps to maintain strong eye contact and to communicate with my body language that they should get ready and pay attention.

The use of a brief pause at the end of a dramatic section of the story can also give time for the importance of what has just happened to sink in. It allows some space for listeners to feel emotions before moving on. Also, pausing at the end of a scene can help listeners transition with you, to close that segment of the story in their minds and clear the slate for a new scene.

Using Movement

Embodied storytelling—using movement—begins before the first words are even spoken. We embody the persona of the storyteller as we walk to the front of the sanctuary and look out at the listeners in the moments before we begin. We are playing a role from that first moment—the role of narrator. By the way we hold ourselves, we communicate that this story will be worth listening to.

Once we begin the story, our posture, facial expressions, eye contact, and movements all become part of how we embody a character or action. That embodiment can range from nonexistent to subtle, to lively, or even to over-the-top distracting. How lively or subtle we are should fit the particular story we are telling. Even over-the-top can be appropriate if the nature of the story is playful

59

and larger than life. But that same over-the-top energy can trample the delicacy of other stories.

Embodied Telling

Embodied telling starts with being present in one's own body, using good posture and direct eye contact, and feeling comfortable in one's own skin, or at least pretending to. An embodied storyteller chooses which actions to portray through movement to emphasize key actions or moments in the story. Subtle movements that signal or intimate action that listeners experience more fully through their imagination work best. The teller can make small changes in posture, stance, and movement to portray various characters, and when appropriate to the story, adopt larger-than-life movements.

Movements That Overwhelm or Distract

Storytelling is always a collaboration between how the story is rendered by the teller and how listeners bring the story to life through their imagination. With exceptions, too much movement or overly dramatic movement prevents the listener from imagining the story. Large movements are fine and may fit in even a relatively delicate story. However, using large movements for the sake of using them is a common mistake often born of anxiety that the story or the teller will not be able to hold listeners' attention. Some tellers want to draw too much attention to themselves rather than to the world and characters of the story. Regardless of motivation, ill-fitting large movements can distract from listeners' experience of living the story. Similarly, too many movements can distract listeners. If everything in the story is mimed, the important moments and corresponding relevant movements get lost in a sea of motion.

Disembodied Telling

Some tellers may feel awkward when trying to add movement to their telling of a story. They may be more comfortable without any movement. Many listeners, however, are predominantly visual people. They may need to see the story to help it come alive in their minds. If movement feels awkward to you at first, begin by adding subtle movements. Rehearse in front of a mirror. Repetition of the movement you are using will help your body to move more automatically and naturally. You will grow accustomed to the experience of showing the story through movement,

Practice

Embodying a Story

Try adding subtle movement to the following section of "The Keeper of the Rain." You will find it useful to practice in front of a mirror so that you can see the impact of your movements.

> *She heard splashing coming from the pond.* [as you say the next line, use your hands to separate the imaginary cattails as the Keeper tilts her head to peer through them] *She peered through the cattails and saw him standing knee-deep in the water.* [as you read the next line, bend slightly and thrust your arms downward as if into the pond water] *The boy bent over and plunged his hands to the bottom of the pond.* [next, straighten from your subtly bent position and bring your hands up in front of your abdomen with your armful of muck] *He stood up with an armload of muck and a wriggling crayfish.*

Read through the rest of the story, looking for moments you want to highlight with subtle yet engaging movements. Remember to avoid the extremes of acting out everything or standing stiffly, using no movement.

As you choose your deliberate movements to embody the story, remember to let extraneous movements fall away. Resist movements that don't advance the story, often born of nervousness. Simply let your arms and hands rest at your sides, and let your voice and face carry the story in those moments when you are not intentionally using movement.

and with time, you will feel less awkward. Ultimately, feeling more comfortable in your body as a storyteller will improve your overall presence and the ease with which listeners engage with the stories you tell.

Developing Characters

Developing nuanced characters in your telling is a powerful way to draw the listener deeper into your story. It is also challenging. Whereas most plays, films, or television productions have multiple actors, storytelling has only one. The storyteller must develop the ability to portray a broad range of characters. Subtle differences in characterization take on new importance. If there is no change in character, listeners might become confused about who is talking or acting in a particular scene. If the difference in characterization is too heavy-handed, listeners may be distracted by the shifts or the characters may not seem genuine. Unbelievable characters pull readers out of the story.

There are a number of ways to subtly indicate a change in character. Often, one or two subtle shifts will subconsciously register in listeners that you have changed roles. Using the upper versus the lower register of your own voice subtly tells listeners that you are speaking for different characters. Facing one direction, then shifting to face a slightly different direction intimates a conversation between two people. A small change in facial expression or a shift from raised eyebrows to pursed lips can symbolize a shift from one character to another. One character might speak slowly, another character slightly quicker. Having a clear sense of the character in your own mind will help you consistently convey differences to your listeners.

Inviting Emotion: A Doorway to Pathos

The goal of storytelling is not to show emotion through the characters in the story or to even experience the emotions as a teller. Rather, the goal is to open a window into a story so that *listeners* can access their own emotions. In storytelling, we are not reaching for the perfect portrayal of emotion; we are reaching for a portrayal of a

┌─ Practice ────────────────────────

Developing Characters

Read through the following sections of "The Keeper of the Rain," paying attention first to the character of the rock. How can you use your own voice to intimate that of the rock? Can you use your voice to hint at that "low-rumbling way of rocks"? How do you experience the rock's personality? Calm, patient, ironic, wise, or resigned? Are there subtle ways to show that with your face? Play with the character until you find what feels true to the story and your own range of expression. Practice in front of a mirror to see the characterization.

> *Many such days passed. As the boy lay basking in the sun, the rock asked, "Have you noticed, the trees and plants are turning yellow?" The boy sat up and looked. "I like the color yellow," said the boy. "They need rain," said the rock. "I don't like rain," said the boy. "I know," said the rock.*

> *Many more such days passed. As the boy lay basking in the sun, the rock asked, "Have you noticed, the trees and plants are turning brown?" The boy sat up and looked. "I like the color brown," said the boy. "They need rain," said the rock. "I don't like rain," said the boy. "I know," said the rock.*

Next, focus on the character of the boy. How might the boy's voice subtly differ from the voice of the rock or your narrator voice? How do you imagine the boy's personality? Do you find him excited, playful, skeptical, distracted, innocent, disaffected, or something else entirely? Are there subtle ways to show that demeanor with your face? Play with the character until you find what feels true to the story and your own range of expression.

Finally, read through the sections while switching from the characterization of the rock to the characterization of the boy to your usual narrator voice. In what subtle ways can you help the listener follow the dialogue and imagine the characters?

story and its characters that opens up the listeners' own emotional response. We do this best by subtly showing emotion rather than over-emoting.

Over-emoting takes the act of emotional interpretation away from the listener and reduces rather than deepens the emotional impact of the story. As listeners and readers, we are naturally suspicious of someone trying to make us feel one way or another. If someone is working too hard or exaggerating, not only are we distracted, but we might also feel that we are being manipulated. We resist the very emotion the teller is trying to elicit. Or we might minimize the emotion we feel, thinking that the events aren't really that sad or that scary.

My perspective as a storyteller is that the listener has to be engaged in the work of making the story come alive. I want the listeners to get the story, and I do everything in my power to tell it well, including significant rehearsal and an openness to learning how to tell it better. In the end, however, it is up to each listener. This attitude helps me to avoid over-acting and over-reaching, and therefore undermining the story and my telling.

At the same time, we do not want to be totally flat or emotionless. Reading or telling a story as a robot would likely make it difficult for listeners to engage with the story. The story needs some expression so listeners can begin to imagine for themselves what is happening and why it is important. Characters must be convincingly human (or humanlike if anthropomorphized) to evoke a sense of caring.

Ideally, we allow the actions, relationships, and events of the story to create an opportunity for an emotional reaction in the listeners. We use subtle changes of voice, facial expression, and body language. We do not tell the story as if it did not matter, but we tell it in a restrained enough way to leave room for a heartfelt reaction. We leave space before and after emotional points of the story that allow the listeners that necessary sliver of time to feel the impact of those key points.

Communicating and Inviting Emotions through Storytelling

Read aloud the following paragraph from "The Keeper of the Rain." As you read, identify the emotions that the boy and the rock are feeling. Experiment with different levels of expression. Try varying your tempo, volume, pitch, facial expression, movement, and dramatic pauses to heighten the emotional weight of the passage. Feel for a level of emotion that opens the door for the listeners' own emotions without overwhelming them with a display of your own.

> *Many more such days passed, and as the boy lay basking in the sun, the rock asked, "Have you noticed, you have to walk farther to get to your pond?" The boy sat up and looked.* [include a short dramatic pause] *"Who moved my pond?"* [practice changing your voice, facial expression, tempo to communicate a subtle sense of alarm or surprise] *asked the boy. "No one," said the rock. "The pond is shrinking. It needs rain."* [contrast the boy's subtle alarm with the rock's steady emotionally even tone] *The boy sat and listened. "It's too quiet,"* [practice changing your voice, facial expression, tempo to communicate a subtle sense of suspicion or concern] *said the boy. "The frogs aren't peeping." "Frogs cannot live without rain," said the rock. "Nothing can."* [without overdoing it, allow a slight gravitas to convey these words]

Using a voice or video recorder can be particularly helpful in listening more objectively to one's own emotional expression when telling a story. Or you can enlist a partner and get feedback from one another about the level of emotional accessibility and expression.

Putting It All Together

Attention to each of these aspects, whether you are reading, preaching, or telling a story, will open up a rich, imaginative experience for the listener. Of course, trying to control all of these aspects of delivering a story (voice, volume, tempo, elasticity, rhythm, movement, emotional range) at once can be intimidating. At first, you may be able to concentrate on and adjust only one aspect of your telling at a time. With experience, your awareness of how you are telling a story will come more naturally. Your ability to think and perceive from the listener's perspective will grow with practice. And with adequate preparation, you will be able to incorporate each of these elements into a whole cohesive story.

The Island and the Moon

When the moon turned her face toward the earth, it seemed as if the whole earth shimmered in her silvery light. The moon shined upon the great mountains, and every pebble glowed. She shined upon the vast waters, and every drop of spray glowed. She shined upon the big shore, and every grain of sand glowed. She shined upon the many islands along the coast, and every island glowed, except one. There, nestled close to shore, was one tiny dark island, the only dark spot on the whole shimmery earth.

"Little island," called the moon. "Why do you not glow? Is my light too dim?" The island did not answer, so the moon turned her face more fully to the earth. Still, the island did not glow. "Little island," called the moon. "Are you in shadow?" The island did not answer, so the moon took a deep breath and blew away any wisps of cloud. Still, the island did not glow.

"Little island," called the moon. "Please, tell me, why do you not glow?" Finally, the little island answered. "I am alone," it said.

"You are not alone," said the moon. "The vast waters surround you. See them shimmer in my light."

"The waters are not like me," said the island. "They are not land. I am alone."

"You are not alone," said the moon. "You are but a stone's throw from the big shore."

"I cannot throw a stone and I cannot touch the land," said the island. "I am alone. And alone, I am too little to glow."

"You are not too little to glow," said the moon. "I shine on everything equally—every rock on the great mountain, every drop of spray on the big waters, every grain of sand on the big shore, and every little island." But nothing the moon said could change the island's mind. It still did not glow.

As the moon moved past the little island and watched the dark spot grow smaller and smaller in the distance, she had an idea. The moon called to the waters, "Oh, shining waters, follow me. Follow me." Slowly, slowly, the waters of the little bay slipped out into the ocean. Slowly, slowly, the beach of the big shore stretched closer and closer toward the island. Slowly, slowly, the beach of the little island stretched closer and closer toward the big shore. Slowly, slowly, until they touched. For a few moments, the little island and the big shore were one. And then, slowly, slowly, the waters slipped back into the bay.

When the moon came around again the next night, bringing the waters with her, she shined upon the great mountains, and every pebble glowed. She shined upon the vast waters, and every drop of spray glowed. She shined upon the big shore, and every grain of sand glowed. She shined upon the many islands along the coast, and every little island glowed. The whole earth shimmered in her silvery light.

—by Kristin Maier

CHAPTER 4

The Art of Preparation

Storytellers can learn and master delivery techniques that bring listeners to the edges of their seats. They can choose stories with the power to open hearts and brush up against the sacred. But even with the best stories and all of the available expertise, they cannot be successful without practice and preparation. Whatever one's methods, there are no shortcuts to a well-prepared story. Marie Shedlock, one of the most renowned storytellers of the twentieth century, writes in *The Art of Story-Telling* that the "capacity for work, and even drudgery, is among the essentials of story-telling." Working hard and pushing through moments of drudgery in our preparation will allow our actual telling to be fluid, natural, and anything but drudgery for both teller and listeners.

Once we feel ready to tackle the process of learning to tell a story, there are two main approaches demonstrated in this chapter. One is a process of memorizing carefully chosen words. The other is to memorize the structure and allow extemporaneous language to arise at the time of telling. We can also combine these methods so that the words of particular sections are memorized and others delivered extemporaneously. Whichever method is chosen, if a story is to be told rather than read, it must be learned "by heart."

Structuring Preparation Time

The length of time necessary for preparation depends upon a variety of factors. These include the length and difficulty of the story, the method used for learning it, the rate at which your mind absorbs a story, and your own experience with storytelling and public speaking. In other words, you can't know precisely until you try. I typically start learning a new story a week before the performance. If I won't have six or seven days over which to spread my rehearsal, I usually reconsider my ability to tell the story. If I will be telling a story I have told in the recent past, or one that I have told frequently, I tend to need less time to prepare. However, starting several days beforehand is still necessary for my own creative process. First-time storytellers should allow extra time to prepare and practice to ensure confidence and ease of telling. With experience, the amount of time needed to prepare a story lessens. You will gain a sense of how much time you need and which preparation methods are most effective for you. However, try to avoid cramming for a storytelling. Generally, confident, creative storytelling does not respond well to cramming.

Building reliable pathways in the brain, whether memorizing lines or embedding scenes in your memory, requires frequent repetition over a period of time. People vary in how they engage and retain a narrative. My own process requires that I spend time living in a story, which works best when I leave time to reflect on the story and allow my subconscious mind to sit with it. Over a typical week of preparation, I may spend an hour or less each day rehearsing, yet I find those seven hours are more effective when spread out over the week than if I had spent seven hours in a row practicing the day before. It also allows me to concentrate on the story intensely for short periods of time, a level of concentration that is difficult to sustain for hours on end.

The first day or two of rehearsal with a new story is always the most difficult. It is essential to trust that, over the course of the week, the story will become easier and easier to tell. Initially, however, it takes much work and repetition to gain traction with a new story. Focusing on just the small piece of the story in front of you at the moment is the best way to gain that traction. Don't let the fact that you cannot yet tell the whole story overwhelm your ability to learn the little part of the story you're working on.

As you gain traction and become able to tell the story as a whole, take time to practice in front of a mirror, a friend, a small audience, or a video camera. Make sure to practice telling the story from beginning to end even if, or perhaps especially if, you make an error, skip something, or tell some element in a way you dislike. You can always go back and practice that key part more later, after you finish telling the story as a whole. When you are in front of a congregation or classroom, you will want to keep the story flowing even when you tell some piece differently than you would have liked. Ideally, your listeners will have no idea that anything went wrong.

Some storytellers warn of practicing too much. They argue that practicing deadens a telling. While that might be true for some, my experience has been exactly the opposite. If my telling begins to feel "dead," my solution has always been to practice a little more and delve deeper into the story. Repetition allows me to remove my own stumbling blocks or distractions and intentionally seek the lively, emotional core of the story.

The lived experience of telling a story in front of an actual congregation or audience can also feel different from the practice leading up to it. When the story starts to flow easily in rehearsal, I do not stop my preparation. I have learned to account for the nervous energy and prepare beyond what feels comfortable when I am performing only for myself or another person. The extra repetitions of the story help me to feel confident in my telling, free up more of my brain to be in the moment with the audience, and think less about consciously controlling what I am telling and why.

Performance and Worship

I have heard some ministers and others express dismay when performance is mentioned in relationship to worship. We should be leery of equating worship with performance but we are misguided if we think performance has no place in worship or in storytelling. Performance, if it means careful preparation in order to present a work of art in an effective and moving way, is already an essential part of creating quality worship. How many musicians or pianists perform a piece of music that they have not rehearsed for a significant amount of time? Usually, those who preach, sing, play, read, and even simply facilitate in worship have put significant effort into performing those functions well. We hope that our effort through performance creates an opportunity for those in the congregation to more fully experience the holy.

In reference to storytelling, some have suggested that those telling a story need not prepare or should not worry about performing the story as best they can. It is true that some very enjoyable and meaningful storytelling can be created in worship with participants who need little or no preparation. Volunteers can be asked on the fly to read lines or act out elements of a scene. The improvisational nature of these moments can make worship lively and fun. However, presenting consistently compelling and nuanced storytelling requires rehearsal, preparation, and careful attention to the performance of the story.

Some of the concern about mistaking performance for worship comes from associating performance with gratifying the self as a performer. If performance is experienced as merely the execution of a skill with the desire to direct attention to the self, then performance does not fit with the larger goal of worship—uniting the self with others and the divine. Putting your best effort into preparing a performance as part of worship can be a deeply spiritual experience if done with the right intention. Seriously preparing any art for the purpose of worship can be an opportunity to forego the centrality of the self. The ego's needs are pushed aside in pursuit of art and for the benefit of the congregation/audience.

When the desire for self-acclaim gets in front of the story, the effect is invariably distracting. Good storytelling happens when the storyteller takes the audience somewhere, not when the audience is overly aware of the storyteller during the telling. In truly magical storytelling, the storyteller disappears for a period of time because the audience is busy living in the story. Ideally, only after the story has been told might the audience have a sense of the storyteller's art. Often, they will leave thinking it was just a great story.

A common concern among those who contribute their gifts to worship is that too much focus on the quality of performance will encourage an atmosphere of criticism. We should be cautious about evaluating what anyone offers in worship with the critical air employed in arenas outside of religious life. Our challenge is not to see those who perform only as performers, or professionals only as professionals, but to see all presenters as whole human beings. Although our roles are important, and we have to make judgments about what is appropriate for our worship time together, we strive to always remember that each of us is more than our roles. It is right to ask, "To what extent do we accept the best that people have to offer in our worship service as a true gift from their person to our community?"

What any of us offers need not be perfect, nor more than our genuine, honest effort. Perhaps most important, we do not need to be anything or anyone other than who we are. When we bring our best to storytelling in worship, through preparation and a loving spirit, we can create a deep, joyful, moving worship experience for ourselves and the congregation.

Respect for each person involved in creating a worship experience, whether storyteller, reader, preacher, or musician, must be simultaneously held with respect for the communal nature of our time together. When a congregation graciously allows us to perform a story, a piece of music, or other art form in worship, the attention of the congregants is also a gift to be respected and appreciated. Performance in worship then can be a mutually gratifying, deeply relational way to create sacred space and deepen our sense of communion with one another and that which we know as divine.

How to Begin: Living in the Story

There is no substitute for deep engagement with a story you hope will move others. Begin by rereading the story, simply to enjoy it yourself. Read it without any thought or concern about how you will tell it later; simply experience it as fully as you can. Let the story light up your brain. See it. Hear it. Feel it. Allow yourself to react emotionally. In other words, have an authentic experience of the story.

You likely already have lived in the story at least once, when you first encountered it and thought it might be worthy of telling. Yet we experience a story slightly differently the second, third, or umpteenth time we encounter it, in part because stories resonate with our lived experience, and we amass experiences throughout our lives. Also, a well-written story holds subtle shades of meaning that continue to reveal themselves. Entering a story repeatedly allows us to deepen our own experience of that story, priming us to provide the kind of telling through which others will find their own deep experiences.

After reading the story several times, live with it for a day or two and sleep on it. This requires choosing a story far enough in advance before you begin your week, or weeks, of preparation. Life's demands may not always give you this luxury, but your telling and your listeners' experience will always benefit if you allow deep conscious, and even subconscious, engagement with the story before you begin addressing the mechanics of how to tell it.

As detailed in chapter 2, select a story you genuinely like with enough substance to engage you deeply. Living in a story for a week or longer will be difficult if you are not genuinely connected with it. No matter how well the story fits the themes or motif of the worship service, no matter how much the underlying moral of the story fits what you are trying to teach, if you do not genuinely experience it as a good story, this process will be tedious, and that experience of tedium will likely leak out during your telling.

Begin to imagine the individual characters that appear in the story. What is your gestalt sense of each of them? How do they speak? Move? Appear? What are they wearing? What expressions appear on their faces as they move through the events of the story? What internal and external emotional states do they experience? Live with the characters you will be portraying.

Imagine the physical place where the story unfolds. See the landscape, note the buildings, roads, weather, whatever makes the story feel like a real experience. Let it come alive in your mind. Spend time contemplating what happens in the story. What is your emotional reaction to each development or plot twist?

Once the story is richly planted in your own imagination and psyche, read through it with the goal of identifying the elements that will shape how you will tell it. Listen for the tempo your own reading naturally lends to the story. How does this particular story flow as you experience it? Does it carefully feel its way forward like a person inching through the dark? Does it rush through like a rollicking adventure?

Does it mosey on like the laid-back current of a lazy river? How do you experience its emotional tone? Is it delicate and tender? Is it raucous or gently playful? Is it poignant and weighty?

Answering these questions will help you develop a fitting tone for the story as a whole. How you inhabit the role of narrator will impact the tone and how it fits with the story as well. The narrator is sometimes so subtly characterized that the listeners are barely aware of the teller in that role. At other times, the narrator is more apparent and distinct. Either way, from your very first words, you will be building the character of the narrator. As you read through the story, listen for the narrator's voice. Is the narrator earnest? Sly? All wise? Silly? Your answer to that question will help you develop the story with the overall tone, tempo, and voice in mind.

Bringing Life (But Not Too Much) into the Story

Once you have fully lived and experienced the story, you must decide which of the imagined elements to fully express through your telling. If you described in words every detail you felt, saw, touched, and heard in your own experience of the story, even a short story would take up the entire worship hour. Make the story come alive but in a way that does not overburden the listener with details. Whole worlds can be intimated with very few words, and generally should be.

A Thin Story

A story that is too thin does not include enough detail to draw listeners in. A thin story does not offer verisimilitude, the sense that the story is real. Shallowly drawn characters come across as flat, lifeless symbols rather than people we can imagine existing. If the story does not adequately engage the senses, listeners can sometimes have difficulty entering the story. People have a tremendous capacity to suspend disbelief and imagine, if only for a moment, that the impossible is possible and the unreal, real. If, after suspending our disbelief, we cannot enter a story as momentarily real, it loses its power. Even fanciful stories should have enough detail to bring the story alive as if it could have happened if we had lived once upon a time.

An Overcrowded Story

Storytelling becomes strained when too much physical description interrupts the sense of timing of actions and events. Too much detail can be difficult to sort through and will likely disrupt the pace of the story so that it cannot be experienced in real time. When you impart every detail to your listeners, you forget that the primary canvas for storytelling is not your imagination, but theirs. Additionally, you have likely created a confused canvas that distracts listeners from the most important artistic and narrative details.

A Good Thick Story

An appropriately thick story gives enough detail to make the story feel like actual lived experience for the listeners without obstructing the wholeness of the story. Such a story opens the door to engage the listener's imagination. The story gives listeners a sense of place that they can visualize and step into. The world of the story can at times be seen, heard, touched, tasted, and smelled. Characters seem real enough to have actually lived. Small details intimate a larger whole without bogging down the narrative in excessive detail. The story feels full, without compromising tempo and pacing.

If you tell a story word for word without changing any of the language, you will not need to decide how much detail to include. Pick a story that is written with an appropriate level of detail to engage the audience. You might retell some stories with subtle additions to enhance the degree to which the story comes alive for listeners. Similarly, some retold stories benefit greatly by strategically omitting extraneous details and lines. As a storyteller, you will need to make these critical artistic choices.

Choosing a Method for Learning and Telling

Once you have lived in a story, and it is alive in your imagination, you are ready to begin learning it for telling. There are two main approaches to learning and retelling

76

a story. One method relies on memorization of specific language. The other relies upon memorizing visual "scenes" and allowing the language to be chosen in the moment of telling. Some storytellers use a variety of methods depending upon the type of story they are telling, and others use a combination of memorized and free-flowing language in the telling of a single story.

Both methods have extensive traditions to draw from, each with its particular strengths, and each its potential pitfalls. Try both or a combination of the two to understand which way of learning a story works best for you. How you best learn and tell a story is related to the structure of your mind and your strengths and comfort as a storyteller.

Learning Scene by Scene
When learning a story scene-by-scene, don't concern yourself too much with the specific words you will use to describe the scenes. It's more important to describe each scene as if you remember it as a whole authentic experience. Create a strong visual and sensory memory of the story as if you have watched or lived it. The language you use flows naturally as if you were in conversation with someone.

The beauty of the scene-by-scene method is that it is relational. It emphasizes flexibility, which more easily encourages spontaneous interaction between the teller and the audience. At its best, this style engenders an in-the-moment quality and leads to a lively experience for audience and teller.

There are also potential pitfalls to this method. Since the teller doesn't labor at memorizing all the words, it can seem that this method doesn't require much time or work to prepare. Yet the lack of solid preparation and rehearsal can prevent precision of language, movement, and nuance. While the teller searches for words in the moment, the audience might hear a lot of distracting "ums," "ers," and "then . . . then . . . thens." Listeners can get distracted and pulled out of the story by their anxiety for the teller and the teller's ability to complete the story.

In the end, whether learning visually or verbally, the teller must still remember and tell the story. Just because the teller has not memorized words doesn't mean he or she can't forget key elements of the story. Ways to cope with such missteps are detailed near the end of this chapter. Ultimately, however, preparation is the surest way to offer the best telling of a story.

Learning Word for Word

When learning a story word for word, the teller seeks to relate the story using language that has been carefully chosen and rehearsed for a consistent effect. The language may already have been chosen by another author, or the teller may be choosing the language as part of preparing the story. Thorough preparation minimizes deviation from the most effective language the teller has found to communicate the story.

The key to memorizing language is, of course, repetition. Break up the story into paragraphs, repeating the first line of the first paragraph until it flows smoothly. Repeat the next sentence until it too flows smoothly. Then repeat these sentences together. When you can speak easily and naturally—not as if you have memorized the lines—keep adding sentences until you can repeat the whole paragraph well enough that it sounds conversational. Learn each paragraph this way and then repeat them with the previous portions of the story until the entire story flows naturally and seamlessly as a whole.

The beauty of the word-for-word method is that the language can be carefully chosen and practiced for consistency of telling. Because you plan and practice ahead of time, you can deliberately choose and strengthen the nuances of the language. You can cue movements, facial expressions, and pauses to specific words for precise timing in the story. And, because the path of the telling is set, you are less likely to deviate in unhelpful and unplanned ways.

There are also potential pitfalls to the word-for-word method. If you practice and perform the story in a rote way, the telling will sound lifeless and canned. Merely reciting words does not produce effective storytelling. The story should be told in a way that is engaging and full. This method permits less flexibility in the telling, so you might have more difficulty responding to the unexpected. Interruptions can present a challenge, as you attempt to find your place again. And you must be prepared for a failure of memory. Again, the end of this chapter offers strategies for coping with these situations.

Combining Spontaneous Language and Deliberate Language

Some storytellers use a combination of memorizing words and learning visual scenes. Many choose to memorize the beginning of the story so that if they get nervous, they can rely on the right words being readily available. Many storytellers memorize the final paragraph or ending of the story to be certain it ends in a particular nuanced way. Even if they include variation in the middle, they are confident they can bring the story home to its rightful end. Some storytellers memorize a particularly important line or section to ensure that they stick to particular language or a particular way of telling. It is likely that most storytellers use one method or another predominantly. However, methods can vary based on the style of story or setting. For example, a story with audience participation may work better without preset lines. A particularly delicate emotional story, one with a rhyming structure, or one that is well known to others might require sticking to the original language.

Doing What Works for You

There is no one right way to learn a story, although plenty of practitioners of any art form will tell you that their way is the only legitimate one. In truth, how we learn best varies significantly from person to person. Some great storytellers memorize language and others choose language on the fly. Rather than debate the merits of one method over the other, consider instead the effect that any person's actual storytelling has on listeners. How are those in our worship services affected by our stories and how we tell them? What relationships are built in the process of telling and hearing a story together? What method or methods help you as a storyteller to experience storytelling as an art form that feeds your soul and allows you to feed the souls of others? These questions are far more important than the spurious claim of one superior storytelling method. If a particular method works for you and for your audience, you need not defend it.

My journey with storytelling began with learning stories through visual scenes. My stories were well received using this method, and I found the process enjoyable. During one worship service, I retold the story "Frederick" by Leo Lionni. Within that story is a poem that I needed to learn word for word. I was intimidated by the prospect of memorizing even this bit of poetry. I did learn it, however. I found that in order to render it properly, I had to simply repeat, repeat, repeat, and then repeat some more.

I happened to tell that story the weekend after the flooding in New Orleans. I had chosen it weeks before, because my sermon was to address the human and spiritual value of the arts. After watching in horror as the events of Hurricane Katrina played out, I stood before the congregation reciting, "Who scatters snowflakes? Who melts the ice? Who spoils the weather? Who makes it nice?" I couldn't help but think of the planet's environmental degradation and the looming specter of climate change as I asked aloud, "Aren't we lucky the seasons are four? Think of a year with one less . . . or one more!"

A playful little children's story took a serious and poignant turn. Something about having memorized those words, the fact that I could call them up precisely, allowed me to focus on the emotional weight buried within them. From that moment on, I no longer believed that there was only one way a storyteller should tell a story.

I sought out more heartfelt stories, and I found myself memorizing the words as a way to free more of my mind to attend to their emotional content. I still sometimes tell certain stories with more focus on structure than memorized word choice, especially stories with significant audience participation, like "The Sun Goddess of the Heavens." For delicate stories and those with significant emotional content, I almost always memorize the language.

I would not expect another person to tell a story exactly as I do. The methods I describe here and the examples I offer are meant to be tried on and chosen as they fit you, your learning style, and your particular talents as a storyteller. It is very much an individual choice, but any method requires you to repeat, repeat, repeat, like any art form. In the end, you still have to remember the story fluidly enough so as not to disrupt the telling or make the listeners anxious about your ability to pull it off. Try different methods. Develop your own process and honor it with the gift of adequate time.

Step-by-Step Guide to Telling "The Island and the Moon": Three Methods

"The Island and the Moon" is a good first story for those new to storytelling in worship. At about five hundred words, it is short enough to tackle either word for word or scene by scene. Because the imagery at the beginning and the end of the story is parallel, it is also well suited to using a combination of memorized and free-flowing language.

The following pages offer an in-depth demonstration of how to tell the story using three methods: learning scene by scene, word for word, and a hybrid approach. I show how to break the story into manageable pieces, how to engage the story deeply yourself, how to learn it for telling, and the specific techniques to employ for each part of the story. Even if you already plan to learn the story with one method or another, I recommend reading through both explanations, as each will illuminate different ways of bringing the story to life. Taken together, they offer a detailed account of how to render this story with depth and nuance. Even if "The Island and the Moon" is not a story you would choose to tell yourself, the methods described here can be applied to any story of your choosing.

Learning "The Island and the Moon" Word for Word

If you have not learned a story word for word before, even five hundred words may seem daunting. However, if you can learn one short paragraph by investing an hour, you can learn an entire story in several hours. Once you own the words of that story, your telling can develop powerful nuances that will create a deeply worshipful experience for your listeners. It takes only the investment of time and effort and the ability not to panic at the thought of five hundred words.

To avoid feeling overwhelmed, break the story into manageable pieces. Write one paragraph on an index card and attempt to learn only that. Then go on to the next paragraph. The simple act of writing the language on the card can give your brain a head start toward memorizing the passage.

I have divided "The Island and the Moon" into sections below as I would work with it. You may find that you can absorb more or less in one sitting. It may be less intimidating to have smaller chunks of the story to work with on twice as many cards. I encourage you to do what works for you and, ultimately, for your listeners.

The Island and the Moon: Card #1

When the moon turned her face toward the earth, it seemed as if the whole earth shimmered in her silvery light. The moon shined upon the great mountains, and every pebble glowed. She shined upon the vast waters, and every drop of spray glowed. She shined upon the big shore, and every grain of sand glowed. She shined upon the many islands along the coast, and every island glowed, except one. There, nestled close to shore, was one tiny dark island, the only dark spot on the whole shimmery earth.

Start with just the first card. Begin by reading the first line several times to yourself. Try to repeat it from memory. If the first line is too much to remember, start with the first phrase. Repeat it multiple times from memory and then move on to the second line or phrase. Read this new line word for word several times. Repeat it from memory several times until it begins to flow more naturally. Then, recite the two lines together until the two flow smoothly. Continue in this way, learning and then adding each new line.

It is important very early in the process to memorize not only the words, but also the nuances of your telling. This technique makes the memorization process easier and the memories more deeply rooted. By engaging your body, voice, emotions, and sense memories, you are activating more parts of your own brain in the remembering process, and thus your memories will be more reliable and full. It also makes the rehearsal of the telling more fun than simple recitation.

Every person experiences a story slightly differently and therefore will tell a story slightly differently. Below, I share how I tell the story, but this is not the only way to tell it effectively.

When the moon turned her face toward the earth, it seemed as if the whole earth shimmered in her silvery light.

While speaking the first phrase, "When the moon turned her face toward the earth," I turn my head to scan the audience, to almost subconsciously intimate the moon waxing. I use a subtle hand motion to signify the "shimmering" of light over all of the earth.

The moon shined upon the great mountains, and every pebble glowed. She shined upon the vast waters, and every drop of spray glowed.

I subtly draw out "pebble" and "drop of spray" to emphasize that even the smallest part of creation shimmered under the moon's attention. I make a small arcing motion with my hand, trailing my fingers to indicate the spray.

She shined upon the big shore, and every grain of sand glowed.

As I say "every grain of sand glowed," I hold my index finger and thumb together as if holding a single grain of sand, again drawing out "every grain of sand."

She shined upon the many islands along the coast, and every island glowed, except one.

I slow the tempo as I say "every island glowed" [short pause] "except one." I hold up one finger to emphasize that one, solitary island.

There, nestled close to shore, was one tiny dark island, the only dark spot on the whole shimmery earth.

I use the following effects while reciting this sentence:

There, [short pause to build anticipation for what is wrong or unexpected in the story] *nestled close to shore,* [ever so brief pause] *was* [drawing out the next few words] *one tiny dark island, the only* [draw out "only"] *dark spot on the whole shimmery earth.* [Draw out "whole shimmery earth," but do not repeat the shimmery motion to emphasize that the island is not glowing.]

Continue to work with each line until you are reasonably satisfied with how you are telling it. Experiment with your tone, tempo, voices, movement, emotion, and expression until your telling feels true to you. Once you like how you are telling it, practice the line until it flows smoothly, as if you had not memorized the language but are simply telling it. Follow this process for each new line until you are able to tell the whole section in a way that feels true and flows easily.

The Island and the Moon: Card #2

"Little island," called the moon. "Why do you not glow? Is my light too dim?" The island did not answer, so the moon turned her face more fully to the earth. Still, the island did not glow. "Little island," called the moon. "Are you in shadow?" The island did not answer, so the moon took a deep breath and blew away any wisps of cloud. Still, the island did not glow.

Set aside the first card and turn your attention fully to the second card. As with the first card, begin by repeating the first line, or if that is too much, the first phrase. Then repeat it from memory, or as much of it as you can. Step by step, add phrases or sentences until you have learned the whole section.

If you find that you must animate each line or phrase with tempo, characterization, emotion, movement, or other techniques, before you can memorize it, then do so. If it works best to plant the memory of the whole section in your mind before returning to animate the telling, then take that approach. Make the learning method fit how you learn best, but make sure to infuse the memorized language with life early in the process.

> *"Little island," called the moon. "Why do you not glow? Is my light too dim?"*
>> Spend some time finding the moon's voice. When I tell the story, the moon's voice is slightly more breathy and subtly more ethereal than my narrator voice. I create this difference by using my throat more and making my voice almost imperceptibly higher.

84

I continue to leave lots of space between the words. The tempo of the story is delicate and curious, but not rushing. I leave space after the first question, "Why do you not glow?" and again after the second question to signify that the Moon is truly curious; she is hoping for an answer. The pause should be long enough to allow the audience to wonder what the island will say, but not so long that they become aware of the pause.

The island did not answer, so the moon turned her face more fully to the earth. Still, the island did not glow.

    I use the motion of my head turning as I say, "so the moon turned her face more fully to the earth," and I move my hand to add greater emphasis. I also add a slight pause after "still" to create mild suspense.

"Little island," called the moon. "Are you in shadow?"

    Again, I move between the narrator's voice and that of the moon, and leave a brief space after the question to signify the moon's actual interest and to leave just enough time for the audience to wonder if the island will answer.

The island did not answer, so the moon took a deep breath and blew away any wisps of cloud. Still, the island did not glow.

    After saying, "so the moon took a deep breath," I take a deep breath and blow away the imaginary clouds in a sweeping motion and then say, "and blew away any wisps of cloud." I use my face as the face of the moon.

I am careful to keep the emotional tone of this section very even while saying that the island did not answer and did not glow. I understand the moon as being concerned about the island's darkness but not disappointed, sad, or irritated. Overreaching emotionally in this section would make the emotional content unbelievable.

When you can tell the second section of the story in a truthful way, and it flows reasonably well, return to the first section. Review it until you are able to tell it from memory. Then add the second section. Practice telling these two sections as one whole until they flow well enough that you can focus on how you tell it rather than just recalling the words.

The Island and the Moon: Card #3

"Little island," called the moon. "Please, tell me, why do you not glow?" Finally, the little island answered. "I am alone," it said.

"You are not alone," said the moon. "The vast waters surround you. See them shimmer in my light."

"The waters are not like me," said the island. "They are not land. I am alone."

In this section of the story, an important emotional shift takes place as the moon moves from mild curiosity to concern. The island finally speaks, and thus we begin to encounter the character of the island and understand its motivations. The central plight of the story lies in the island's emotional experience of feeling alone and separated in some fundamental way from all that surrounds it.

As I prepare this section of the story, I am careful not to overemphasize the island's self-absorption or to portray the island as especially foolish or stubborn. Although the island is being somewhat melodramatic, overplaying the character or its melodrama would undermine the audience's ability to identify with the very human nature of its perspective and feelings.

To establish a distinct character for the island, I slightly shift my voice. While the moon voice resonates more in my throat, the island voice resonates more in my head. I am not using a falsetto or a voice other than my own, but utilizing different parts of my natural voice—enough to signal the character change to the listeners without distracting them.

> *"Little island," called the moon. "Please, tell me, why do you not glow?" Finally, the little island answered. "I am alone," it said.*
>
> In order to communicate the moon's genuine concern for the island, I show a concerned facial expression, including a slight tilt of the head and furrowed brow. I add the following pauses: "Please, [pause with concerned expression] tell me, [brief pause] why do you not glow?"

I leave a significant pause before "Finally," and a brief pause before continuing with "the little island answered" to heighten the anticipation of the island finally speaking.

"I am alone" needs to be delivered with the barest touch of self-importance. We want the listener to believe that the island does indeed perceive itself as alone and is not manipulating the moon. I put a slight emphasis on "I" and a tiny pause before "am alone." I am careful not to overdo it, however.

"You are not alone," said the moon. "The vast waters surround you. See them shimmer in my light."

The tempo picks up slightly here. The moon clearly sees the island's interconnectedness and believes that by simply explaining it, the island will see the truth. Because it isn't emotionally laden for the moon, using a quicker pace here with her explanations will help keep the story moving without compromising other more emotionally nuanced parts.

"The waters are not like me," said the island. "They are not land. I am alone."

The island answers with the same tempo, but slows down slightly for "They are not land," and says "I am alone" with the same deliberate insistence as earlier.

Once you have found a way to tell the third section that feels appropriate and truthful to the story, practice it in this manner until the story flows smoothly. Then practice from the beginning through this point until you can tell the whole story as one piece. If your process is like mine, it will take multiple hours of practice spread over multiple days.

The Island and the Moon: Card #4

"You are not alone," said the moon. "You are but a stone's throw from the big shore."

"I cannot throw a stone and I cannot touch the land," said the island. "I am alone. And alone, I am too little to glow."

This portion of the story continues the back-and-forth exchange between the island and the moon. As much as the moon insists that the island is not alone, the island insists that it is. This repeated dynamic could easily drag down the story, so you must create a rhythm that moves along fairly quickly while maintaining the characters' earnestness.

> *"You are not alone," said the moon. "You are but a stone's throw from the big shore."*
> I speak the line, "You are not alone" with a slight shake of my head and a look of consternation, indicating that the moon genuinely does not see the island as the island sees itself.

> *"I cannot throw a stone and I cannot touch the land," said the island. "I am alone. And alone, I am too little to glow."*
> The island's response remains matter-of-fact, as if its aloneness is indisputable.
> I am careful not to let the tempo of these lines drag.

Continue to add each new section to what you have already learned. You may need to spend some time practicing the transition from one card to the next so that you do not have unnatural pauses between sections. Any pauses that you use should fit the overall flow of the story rather than revealing your method of learning the story.

The Island and the Moon: Card #5

"You are not too little to glow," said the moon. "I shine on everything equally—every rock on the great mountain, every drop of spray on the big waters, every grain of sand on the big shore, and every little island." But nothing the moon said could change the island's mind. It still did not glow.

This section of the story includes a short monologue by the moon that mirrors the opening section of the story. Because these lines repeat what the audience has already heard, they should be delivered at a quicker pace. The audience will recognize the images and process them quicker. A delivery that's too slow will leave listeners with too much time to anticipate the next lines, and they will get bored.

> *"You are not too little to glow," said the moon.*
>> The moon remains befuddled by the island's insistence. I emphasize "not" rather than "too little" in order to maintain that sense of a back-and-forth verbal volley between the moon and the island.

> *"I shine on everything equally—every rock on the great mountain, every drop of spray on the big waters, every grain of sand on the big shore, and every little island."*
>> I keep the tempo up through this repetition, adding a slight emphasis to "rock," "drop of spray," and "grain of sand." When I reach "every . . . little . . . island," I draw out the words to add more emphasis.

> *But nothing the moon said could change the island's mind. It still did not glow.*
>> Here the base tempo slows back down. The back-and-forth is over. The line "It still did not glow" is deliberate, with enough time between the words to reflect the intractability of the situation.

You have now learned more than half the story. Practice telling it up to this point as a whole, continuous story. You will likely find you have gained some traction or a sense of momentum in learning and telling the story thus far.

The Island and the Moon: Card #6

As the moon moved past the little island and watched the dark spot grow smaller and smaller in the distance, she had an idea. The moon called to the waters, "Oh, shining waters, follow me. Follow me." Slowly, slowly, the waters of the little bay slipped out into the ocean. Slowly, slowly, the beach of the big shore stretched closer and closer toward the island. Slowly, slowly, the beach of the little island stretched closer and closer toward the big shore. Slowly, slowly, until they touched. For a few moments, the little island and the big shore were one. And then, slowly, slowly, the waters slipped back into the bay.

This section includes the turning point of the story as the island finally has an experience of feeling connected. As this section is fairly long, you may need to break it into even smaller sections to learn.

As the moon moved past the little island and watched the dark spot grow smaller and smaller in the distance, she had an idea.

> I make a small circle with my hand to indicate the island, and as I speak the line, my hand gradually moves farther and farther away from my body, to intimate the island growing farther and farther away from the moon. I pause briefly after announcing that the moon had an idea in order to build a sense of anticipation.

The moon called to the waters, "Oh, shining waters, follow me. Follow me." Slowly, slowly, the waters of the little bay slipped out into the ocean. Slowly, slowly, the beach of the big shore stretched closer and closer toward the island. Slowly, slowly, the beach of the little island stretched closer and closer toward the big shore. Slowly, slowly, until they touched.

> To emphasize the gradualness and emotional importance of the waters slipping out of the bay, I draw out the words "slowly, slowly" and "closer and closer." I speak the other words at a normal pace. I deliver the climax with more time between each word to allow the audience to hear and experience its importance: "Slowly . . . slowly . . . until . . . they . . . touched."

I use my hands to show the gradual movement of the shore toward the island. I hold one hand about shoulder height with my fingers at a gentle slope, similar to the angle of a shoreline. I gradually move that hand in the direction of my center line as I tell of the big shore stretching toward the island. I hold my other hand the same way and move it gradually toward my center as I tell of the island stretching toward the big shore. Eventually, my fingertips touch.

For a few moments, the little island and the big shore were one. And then, slowly, slowly, the waters slipped back into the bay.

I pause for a brief moment after saying "the little island and the big shore were one" to allow it to sink in. Then, I allow my fingertips to separate and my arms to fall to my sides once again as the waters slip back into the bay.

The Island and the Moon: Card #7

When the moon came around again the next night, bringing the waters with her, she shined upon the great mountains, and every pebble glowed. She shined upon the vast waters, and every drop of spray glowed. She shined upon the big shore, and every grain of sand glowed. She shined upon the many islands along the coast, and every little island glowed. The whole earth shimmered in her silvery light.

The final section of the story brings the resolution. I intentionally use relaxed body language and tone of voice to signal that the tension has been resolved, and the story is ending as it should.

When the moon came around again the next night, bringing the waters with her, she shined upon the great mountains, and every pebble glowed.

The language here mirrors that of the beginning of the story. The listeners are still waiting to hear whether or not the island is now glowing, so although

I don't want the story to drag, I want to hold some of the dramatic tension and thus not rush through this part.

She shined upon the vast waters, and every drop of spray glowed. She shined upon the big shore, and every grain of sand glowed.

I use the same hand motions that I used in the beginning to embody the spray and the grain of sand.

She shined upon the many islands along the coast, and every little island glowed.

I draw out "every . . . little . . . island" to heighten the drama just a bit and help the listeners understand that the little island is indeed glowing now.

The whole earth shimmered in her silvery light.

The tempo slows in the final line much like orchestral music does, to signify that the story is ending. I make eye contact with the listeners, using a slow sweep with my eyes, before returning to my seat. It is a way of holding the relationship with the listeners for a moment longer, of not rushing away or leaving the story and the relationship feeling unfinished. This moment also allows me to nonverbally express appreciation to the audience for their gift of attention.

Practicing the Whole Story

By now, you will have a strong sense of how you want to tell each line of the story. Ideally, you will also have been adding each new section to your telling of the previous sections. Thus, you will find that the beginning sections have gotten easier with each expansion of the story. Practicing the whole story from beginning to end is essential for developing an overall tempo and flow.

Once you can reliably find the words of the story, you can devote more of your attention to making adjustments to your delivery. Continue to practice, and if possible, make a video or audio recording of yourself. Try to experience the recording as objectively as you can. Make adjustments to remove distracting elements or enliven flat moments in your telling.

Learning "The Island and the Moon" Scene by Scene

Begin the process of learning "The Island and the Moon" scene by scene with less structured language by identifying the natural breaks between scenes. There is no right or wrong way to do this. The divisions I use in the model that follows might differ from the divisions you choose. Divide the story in a way that helps you to learn and tell it effectively.

Summary of Scenes

Scene #1: The moon turns her face toward the earth, and everything shines, except one little island.

Scene #2: The moon asks why the island won't glow. Is her light too dim? Is it shadowed by clouds? The island doesn't answer.

Scene #3: "Please, tell me," pleads the moon. The island responds, "I am alone."

Scene #4: The moon tries to convince the island it is not alone. The island insists it is too little to glow. The moon cannot change the island's mind.

Scene #5: The moon moves past the island and gets an idea. She calls the waters to follow her. The waters slip out of the tiny bay. The beach of the island and the shore stretch toward one another and touch.

Scene #6: The moon comes around the earth again and finally everything shines, including the island.

Thinking of the story in terms of scenes will provide an internal structure for your own mind and memory. In the best-case scenario, however, listeners will not be aware of the internal structure but will experience the story as a whole as it flows smoothly from moment to moment. Ideally, you will practice enough that your internal structure does not create distracting gaps in the telling.

Learning Scene #1

To tell this story from a rich visual memory, you must first develop that memory by living within the scene with clarity and depth. You must experience it. Start by reviewing the text. Begin to flesh out the imagery that you experience in the story.

Text	Internal Visual Imagery
When the moon turned her face toward the earth, it seemed as if the whole earth shimmered in her silvery light.	Visualize the face of the moon. See her features, expression, the color of her light. Imagine the earth lit by her silvery light.
The moon shined upon the great mountains, and every pebble glowed. She shined upon the vast waters, and every drop of spray glowed. She shined upon the big shore, and every grain of sand glowed.	Conjure up a picture of each element the moon shines upon. See the mountains, the pebbles, the water, and the spray. Make them as real as possible in your mind. Imagine shape, color, size. Try imagining yourself as the moon moving over a three-dimensional landscape, seeing each element you name in turn.
She shined upon the many islands along the coast, and every island glowed, except one.	Picture the line of islands along the coast shimmering in the moonlight. Notice one little dark spot.
There, nestled close to shore, was one tiny dark island, the only dark spot on the whole shimmery earth.	Zoom in on your image to the one dark island. Notice everything around it shimmering.

Once you have fully explored the scene in your imagination, begin to practice telling the scene in your own words. Use the imagery you have developed in your mind to guide your telling, as if remembering something you've witnessed. Practice telling the scene over and over until it is securely planted in your memory and flows easily.

If you find it challenging to remember all of the elements of the scene that you want to tell, create an aid for your telling. Make a brief cheat sheet of key words to guide your memory of the scene. Create a simple storyboard, a series of small illustrations to help guide your learning process. It need not be fancy—stick figures and symbols will do. It need only remind you of the images you want to convey.

With repetition, the words and images will begin to flow more naturally, and you will be able to turn your attention to how you tell the scene. Observe your own telling in relationship to one of the aspects described below. Experiment with different ways of employing that technique. Once your telling feels true in relationship to that element, turn your attention to another technique. Again, practicing in front of a mirror or making an audio or video recording will give you a fresh perspective on your technique. Of course, your telling does not have to be same with each repetition—you are allowed variation. Nonetheless, you do want to practice enough so that each element feels familiar and your telling flows naturally.

Volume

Practice using a clear, strong voice from the very first words of the story. You will likely be most nervous at the start of the story, so deliberately rehearsing with a confident voice will help you pull it off with an actual audience.

Tempo

Listen to hear if your pacing of the story matches the emotional tone you are trying to establish. If possible, make and listen to an audio recording of yourself telling the scene. Does the story drag or rush? Does it feel comfortable to you as a listener? Listen for places where the tempo should change. Try adding a slight dramatic pause after "every island glowed," and before "except one." Try stretching out your description of that one tiny, dark island to highlight the core dilemma of the story.

Emotional Tone

Try beginning the story with a subtle sense of wonder. As the moon becomes aware that one island does not glow, shift to a sense of mild concern. Your mild surprise will cue the listeners that something unexpected is occurring and begin to spark their curiosity. Be careful not to overplay the emotion while you set the stage of the story.

Movement

Look for the occasional subtle, fitting movements that help listeners imagine what you are telling. Try turning your face as you describe the moon turning her face toward the earth. Experiment with hand motions to indicate glowing or shimmery light. Remember, when you are not deliberately moving, let your hands rest at your side so you won't distract with unintentional movement.

Learning Scene #2

As with the first scene, begin by creating your internal visual imagery of the scene. Pay attention to your emotional reaction, then use that to help you live, remember, and retell the scene.

Text	Internal Visual Imagery
"Little island," called the moon. "Why do you not glow? Is my light too dim?" The island did not answer, so the moon turned her face more fully to the earth. Still, the island did not glow.	In your mind, hear the voice of the moon as she tries to understand the island. See her face and expression. Visualize the moon becoming full as she tries to shine brighter for the island. See the island unmoved, still dark.

"Little island," called the moon. "Are you in shadow?" The island did not answer, so the moon took a deep breath and blew away any wisps of cloud. Still, the island did not glow.

Imagine the moon's quizzical expression deepen with each question. Imagine her blowing away the clouds and the still silent darkness of the island.

Once you have a developed a strong personal experience of the scene, begin practicing just this piece, without worrying about remembering the first part of the story. Practice telling it in your own words until the language flows smoothly. Then turn your attention to employing good storytelling technique to shape your telling so that it feels more and more true.

Characterization

Listen for how you might change your voice slightly when speaking as the moon. How do you imagine the moon's voice sounds? Is it somewhat ethereal? Is it dreamy? Is it kind? Does it embody maternal or paternal warmth? Listen as you tell the story for ways you can slightly shift from the narrator's voice to the voice of the moon. Beware of making too great a shift. A falsetto, a funny accent, or an overly breathless voice would probably be too heavy-handed and distracting for this story. If you cannot find a subtle shift in voice that feels natural, simply use one consistent voice and allow the other cues of the story and your telling to lead the listeners. It is better to undershoot than overshoot.

Tempo

In this scene, I leave a brief pause after the moon asks the island a question. I want to allow the listeners just enough time to begin to wonder if the island will answer, but not enough time that they are aware of that wondering. I leave a slight pause before saying that the island still does not glow. I also leave just a little space between "Still" and "the island" to intimate the feeling that the moon is waiting to see what will happen.

97

Emotional Tone

When I tell the story, I want to evoke in the listeners the same puzzlement and compassion that the moon feels for the island. A furrowed brow and slight tilt of the head when asking the island why it doesn't glow will invite the listeners into that same compassionate wondering. To communicate the emotional flatness of the island, I am careful to keep a relatively emotionless tone when stating that the island still did not glow. That flat tone emphasizes the inscrutable character of the island here at the beginning of the story.

Movement

When the moon turns her face more fully toward the earth, I turn my face and even use a slight motion of my hand to emphasize that turning, as if the moon were waxing to full in front of our eyes. When the moon blows away any wisps of cloud, I take a full breath and blow out with full cheeks while turning my head from right to left, making a whooshing sound as I do. I do not blow out with the hyperenthusiasm of blowing out birthday candles, but with the deliberateness I imagine a giant celestial body would have.

Once you are satisfied with telling the second scene, return to the first scene. Practice telling the first two scenes together as one piece of the story. When telling this story, I find that a short pause between the first and second scenes fits naturally with the story (which is why I chose that breaking point). Practice the two scenes together enough that the pause between them fits the story and does not draw attention to your internal structure.

Learning Scene #3

This scene is very short and may hardly seem worth remembering as its own scene. Yet it is the pivotal turning point in the story. The island, as a character, speaks for the first time and begins to emerge. We have been waiting for this moment: to learn why this little island does not glow.

Text	Internal Visual Imagery
"Little island," called the moon. *"Please, tell me, why do you not glow?"*	Imagine the concern on the moon's face as she tries one last time to find out why the island will not glow.
Finally, the little island answered. "I am alone," it said.	Imagine the little island, its demeanor, its voice, its emotional mood as it makes its solemn announcement.

Characterization
By now, we have met all three characters: the moon, the island, and the invisible narrator. If you have not already found a voice and demeanor for these three roles, try experimenting with slight shifts of your voice, facial expression, even body language. I try to keep the narrator voice as close as possible to my regular public speaking voice, which happens to be centered more in my chest. I make the moon's voice slightly breathier and more in my throat. For the island, I tend to move my voice into my head, allowing the sound to resonate in my skull. These subtle shifts are enough to signal the shift in character in the listeners' imaginations.

Tempo
This important turning point in the story includes an emotional shift, so it can support a slowing of tempo. The listeners will need a little time to take in the

99

moon's emotional shift. They will wonder if, this time, the island will answer. And when the island does finally answer, their psyches will want a moment to absorb what has happened.

Emotional Tone
There must be something in the way the moon implores the island that convinces it to finally speak. I do my best to communicate genuine concern through the moon character. For this section, I intensify that concern a bit more and even emphasize the "please" as if the moon is accepting that the island is holding the cards. She has accepted that she cannot make the island glow and cannot even make it tell her why. Through the island's response, I try to communicate that it genuinely believes it is alone. I am careful not to overplay the emotion and make the island seem insincere or manipulative.

Practice this third scene and its nuances several times. Once it flows smoothly and you are able to tell the story as you live in it, try telling the story from the beginning and flow through into the third scene. If this feels like too much, tell just the second and third scenes until they flow comfortably. Then add the first scene. Practice until the whole story to this point flows appropriately from scene to scene.

Learning Scene #4

The pursuer/distancer dance continues between the moon and the island. The moon tries to demonstrate to the island that it is not alone. The island, convinced of its separateness, parries the moon's insistence.

Text	Internal Visual Imagery
"You are not alone," said the moon. "The vast waters surround you. See them shimmer in my light." *"The waters are not like me," said the island. "They are not land. I am alone."*	Imagine the moon turning her face toward the shimmering waters, as if the islands' connection to the waters was obvious. Imagine the island completely unaffected as if unwilling to be convinced.
"You are not alone," said the moon. "You are but a stone's throw from the big shore." *"I cannot throw a stone and I cannot touch the land," said the island. "I am alone. And alone, I am too little to glow."*	Imagine the moon turning her face toward the big shore, again pointing out the obvious. Again, the island is unconvinced, drawing attention to how small it is.
"You are not too little to glow," said the moon. "I shine on everything equally— every rock on the great mountain, every drop of spray on the big waters, every grain of sand on the big shore, and every little island."	Imagine the moon's beams shining down on all the littlest things from the first scene.
But nothing the moon said could change the island's mind. It still did not glow.	Imagine the moon's looking on helplessly as the island remains dark.

Characterization

This scene requires the teller to move quickly between one character and the other. The moon is invested in helping the island understand itself as part of a greater whole. The island is invested in not having its sense of itself be denied. It sets up an interesting back and forth. I try to represent both characters as honestly holding their own perspective. So I switch back and forth between what feels like the moon's continued concern and gentle insistence and the island's steadfast, earnest insistence upon its own loneliness.

Tempo

To give the impression of a volley of words and reasoning between the moon and the island, I increase the tempo of this section. The actual words and reasoning matter less than the emotional subtext of the island's inability to see its connectedness and the moon's inability to change that perception for the island. Also, this scene uses mirror imagery from the first scene. The listeners have already imagined the moon shining on the pebbles, the spray, the grains of sand, and the other islands. They are ready to imagine them again at a quicker pace. To stay ahead of their conscious awareness of the tempo, you need to tell this section a little more quickly.

Once you have established a solid method for telling this fourth scene, combine it with the first three. After practicing enough to establish a good flow for telling the whole story thus far, turn your attention to how consistently you represent the main characters of the moon, the island, and the narrator. If you embody the characters with subtle shifts in voice or variations in posture, expression, and position of the face, make sure that you do so in a reasonably consistent way throughout the story. You may find that your sense of these characters has changed since you began telling the story, and you may need to make adjustments to the earlier parts.

Learning Scene #5

In this highly visual scene, the island undergoes a physical change. We see what happens as the island comes to touch the shoreline, but we do not learn the effects of that change on the island's self-perception until the next scene. Thus, although something magical is happening, the tension of the story still is not yet fully resolved.

Text	Internal Visual Imagery
As the moon moved past the little island and watched the dark spot grow smaller and smaller in the distance, she had an idea.	Imagine from the moon's perspective watching the little island growing smaller and smaller in the distance. Feel the proverbial lightbulb go off in the moon's mind.
The moon called to the waters, "Oh, shining waters, follow me. Follow me."	Hear the moon calling out to the waters below.
Slowly, slowly, the waters of the little bay slipped out into the ocean. Slowly, slowly, the beach of the big shore stretched closer and closer toward the island. Slowly, slowly, the beach of the little island stretched closer and closer toward the big shore. Slowly, slowly, until they touched.	Watch as the waters slowly flow out of the bay and around the big shore to be pulled toward the moon. Watch as the water gets lower, and the beach of the shore and the beach of the island stretch toward one another and finally touch.
For a few moments, the little island and the big shore were one.	Imagine the pleasure of the little island as it feels being part of something greater than itself.
And then, slowly, slowly, the waters slipped back into the bay.	Watch the water start to fill the bay once again.

Tempo

I stretch the words "slowly, slowly" to give an auditory sense of the gradual nature of the tide. I do, however, say the other words describing what is happening at a slightly quicker pace to avoid boring the listeners. I make sure to slow down and stretch out the moment when the island and the shore touch, to give listeners time to absorb the importance of this moment.

Emotional Tone

In this scene, I like to keep the emotional tone as subtle wonder. I tell this scene with no embellishment and only a relatively subdued if expectant tone. I try to let the action of the waters and the shore speak for themselves.

Movement

In this highly visual scene, I try to use my physical body to intimate what I hope the audience is seeing in their imagination. I hold one hand with my fingers at a gentle slope and gradually move my hand toward my center line to indicate the big shore moving toward the island. I move my other hand gradually toward my center to indicate the beach of the island stretching toward the big shore. Eventually, my fingertips touch, hold together for a moment, and then slowly separate again. This isn't a huge or overt movement. It aims to spark the listener's own visual imagery of watching a tide move out.

Once you are satisfied with how you tell this scene, begin practicing it with the prior scenes. Because you have repeated the earlier scenes many times already, you will likely find it is becoming easier to add each new section. You are almost there.

Learning Scene #6

The concluding scene acts as a bookend with the first scene and its parallel imagery, but this time the problem reaches a resolution. The island finally glows along with the whole shimmery earth.

Text	Internal Visual Imagery
When the moon came around again the next night, bringing the waters with her, she shined upon the great mountains, and every pebble glowed. She shined upon the vast waters, and every drop of spray glowed. She shined upon the big shore, and every grain of sand glowed.	See the moon come around the earth, pulling the tide with her and shining upon each of the parallel elements from the introductory scene. Visualize the pebbles on the mountain, the spray on the waters, each grain of sand on the shore.
She shined upon the many islands along the coast, and every little island glowed. The whole earth shimmered in her silvery light.	Visualize the line of shining islands and imagine in your mind the little island, now shining.

Tempo

This is the third time the story references the pebbles, spray, sand, and islands. Repetition typically calls for speeding up the tempo, but in this section the audience is still waiting to hear if the island will finally glow. In order to make the most of that anticipation, I use a relatively slow pace and a brief dramatic pause before saying that *every* little island glowed.

Emotional Tone

I provide some anticipation for the outcome of the story by having the narrator communicate a sense of joy and triumph as I begin this final section of the story. When I finally say that every island glowed, the listeners experience a sense that everything is again as it should be. I communicate this sense of joy and rightness with a soft smile on my face, careful to still underplay the emotion and leave room for the listeners to experience their own.

Ending the Story

I speak the final words of the story, about the whole earth shimmering, more slowly, and with an air of ending. I make sweeping eye contact, as I am concluding my relationship with the listeners. I hold eye contact and a warm emotional expression for a moment longer before returning to my seat. I don't want to give the impression to those listening that I am rushing away now that the story is done. The relationship between teller and audience is as important as any other element of good storytelling. It will get you invited back to tell another story on another day.

As soon as you have worked through how you will tell the final scene and how you will end the story, you are ready to start practicing it as a whole. Practice in front of a mirror or record your telling to help you apply a more objective ear and eye to how you are communicating the story. Adjust your telling whenever something feels untrue or distracting. Giving careful attention to how you use voice, volume, tempo, movement, and characterization will help you both to learn your story and tell it in an engaging way. Even though this method results in a fluid telling with variations in each performance, consistently rich performances will come from thorough practice of good technique.

Combining Word-for-Word and Scene-by-Scene Methods

"The Island and the Moon" is particularly well suited to using a combination of word-for-word and scene-by-scene telling. The beginning and ending paragraphs use parallel imagery. Memorizing the language to ensure that the imagery is accurate will strengthen listeners' experience of the story having "bookends." The listeners' sense that the story has returned to its original place will be strengthened by the precision of the imagery.

To use a hybrid method, identify the parts of the story in which you want to automatically recall the language. Use the process for learning a story word for word to master those parts of the story. Practice the other parts of the story with the scene-by-scene method. Then practice the story as a whole, making sure to attend to the transition in and out of the memorized sections. Ideally, you'll repeat the process enough in your preparation that the audience will have no awareness of your method but only their lived experience of the story.

Final Preparations

However you have learned your story, careful attention to final preparations will help ensure that the actual telling goes as smoothly as possible. As you gain confidence in telling the story, you may feel that you are done practicing. I encourage you to continue to refresh your telling as you draw nearer to the actual performance. At times, I have experienced a feeling of faux readiness in my preparation. After I tell the whole story through a few times, it begins to flow easily. Early on in my storytelling, I once mistook this early ease with being fully prepared. In reality, I simply had not practiced enough to find my stumbling blocks. I found them during the performance, which was an uncomfortable experience.

My own process requires that I push past this initial ease. As I continue to rehearse the story after it feels comfortable, I find the places where my telling starts to break down. This is often a part of the story that is similar to another part. Or I use language that I feel is not quite right, and I become distracted by my internal artistic tensions. Whatever the reason for the difficulties, they are only overcome by practicing through them. Rather than get discouraged, I accept the revelation of this block as a gift. It helps me to understand where I need to put extra effort.

However comfortable you become with your rehearsal, you will likely tell the story with a different mindset once you are in front of your actual audience. Some degree of nervousness is inevitable if you care deeply about how you tell a story. If you aren't nervous at all, one might wonder if you have forgotten that having an audience's attention is a tremendous gift.

Being nervous about a performance is nearly inescapable and not necessarily negative. It can motivate us to continue preparing. Nervousness keeps us focused even when we are working through a part of the preparation that isn't our favorite. The key is to keep our nerves at a level that is motivating but not debilitating. Remember that in a religious community, you will be loved even if you utterly fail.

To help prepare for the added anxiety during a performance, rehearse each time while imagining that the audience is right in front of you. You can also enlist a dress rehearsal audience of trusted friends or family. Telling the story in front of real people, if not the actual audience, gives you the opportunity to practice with at least some of the game day surge of adrenaline.

Dealing with Inevitable Mistakes

Errors or mistakes in storytelling are inevitable. I don't think I have ever told a story in which I didn't watch something go by that I would have preferred to tell differently, whether I have memorized the language or not. An important part of preparing is anticipating mistakes and planning how to respond. Another part is simply accepting that the telling will not go entirely as planned and to be okay with that before even speaking the first words. Remember that you will be the person most aware of the mistake. Overreacting to small disappointments in the telling only takes away from the listeners' experience.

Creating a Safety Net

To help cope with the inevitable, I recommend that every teller create some kind of safety net for telling a story. It can include a visual aid for telling the story in case you lose your place, perhaps the full text of the story in large print. It might be an outline or a list of key words. It might be a storyboard or perhaps the first line of each paragraph. It should simply guide you in your telling if needed. Even if I never look at it, I keep my text nearby on a music stand, where it is easy to read if I need it.

You can enlist the help of a friend to follow along with the text and feed you a line if needed. You can work out a signal so your friend does not mistake your dramatic pause for a moment of confusion. Ideally would rehearse in front of this friend so that they will be able to recognize if and when you need a cue.

Practice how to respond to losing your place. Instead of being flustered in a way that pulls the audience into your anxiety, practice asking the audience in a calm and relaxed way, "Now where was I?" They will tell you. If you ask in a natural way, as if it happens to you all the time and you always recover, they will not grow anxious for you. It will minimize the disruption of the story.

Ideally, you will not make big errors, but even the best storytellers make them. Handle this situation with humility and a sense of humor. You do not even have to let the audience know you missed something. If the mistake is minor, and they are following the story, keep going. If it is important enough that you need to address it and can do so as if that's how you always tell the story, then great. If you need to say "Oops!" and back up to fix the story, then do so with humor and humility. Our mistakes are an opportunity to remember that we're human and deserve forgiveness from our inner critic as well.

The Sun Goddess of the Heavens

The story of the Sun Goddess, Amaterasu Omikami, is found in the most ancient book of Japan called the Kojiki. This is a collection of ancient Japanese myths compiled by the nobleman no Yasumaro in the eighth century. The roots of the Shinto religion are found in the myths of the Kojiki, an ancient and appreciated source of imagery and meaning for the Japanese people. This retelling is inspired by a version created by Keiko Cauley. Her adaptation retains the most beautiful elements of the story of the Sun Goddess in a way that is well suited for all ages.

Long, long ago, high in the heavens above Japan, was the land of the gods and goddesses.

It was a peaceful land, ruled by the Sun Goddess, Amaterasu Omikami. Amaterasu was a kind and gentle ruler. When she smiled her gentle smile, all the heavens were at peace.

The Sun Goddess had a little brother named Susano no Mikoto. One day, Susano called up to the heavens, "Please, sister, can I come and live up in the heavens with all the gods and goddesses?"

Amaterasu said to her little brother, "If you are to live in the land of the heavens, you must promise to behave and not make any mischief."

"Yes, sister. I promise to behave and not make any mischief." The Sun Goddess smiled her gentle smile, and her little brother climbed up to the land of the gods and goddesses.

Susano was the Sun Goddess's little brother, but he was also a powerful god who liked to play rough and rowdy sometimes. At first, he remembered his promise to his sister, but after a while, he forgot.

Soon he was stomping through the land, wrecking the rice fields and destroying the canals that the other gods and goddesses had built.

But Amaterasu did not worry. "My little brother is just up to some mischief," she said, as she smiled her gentle smile. "I am sure he will not cause any more trouble."

But Susano grew rowdier and rowdier. One day, Amaterasu had gathered the women in the loom house to weave a special cloth for the gods. Suddenly, Susano no Mikoto threw a huge horse's hide onto the loom. The loom broke, sending splinters in every direction. Some of the women were hurt.

Amaterasu was furious. She could no longer smile her gentle smile. She ran to a cave, hid herself inside, and sealed the cave shut with a large boulder. Without the Sun Goddess, the heavens and earth were plunged into darkness.

The other gods and goddesses rushed to the cave. "Sun Goddess," they called, "the world has been plunged into darkness. Please come out and smile your gentle smile." But no sound came from the cave.

The strongest gods and goddesses tried to move the boulder aside. They pushed and they pulled, but they could not make it budge. They needed another plan.

First, they built a giant bonfire. Then, they brought all of the roosters from the land. Finally, they brought a very large mirror. Now they were ready. They began to play music and dance.

Deep inside the cave, Amaterasu heard music and laughter. "How can there be music and laughter when the world has been plunged into darkness?" she wondered. "What is going on out there?" she called from the cave.

"It is the new Sun Goddess," answered the gods. "We are welcoming her."

"The new Sun Goddess?" wondered Amaterasu. She pushed the boulder open a crack.

The roosters saw the crack of light coming out of the cave and thought it was the dawn. "Kokokoko-ro! Kokokoko-ro!"

Curious, Amaterasu pushed the boulder open a bit farther. When she peeked out of the cave, she saw before her the light of a sun goddess. "Beautiful!" she said, not recognizing herself in the mirror. She stepped out from the cave. Just as she did, the strongest god rushed forward and closed the cave behind her.

Everyone cheered and clapped, for the world was no longer plunged into darkness.

"O, Sun Goddess," they all pleaded. "Never plunge us into darkness again." Seeing how much the other gods and goddesses needed her, Amaterasu Omikami forgot her anger and smiled her gentle smile once again.

And her little brother, Susano no Mikoto? He was sent back down to earth for a while to think about what he had done.

—retold by Kristin Maier

CHAPTER 5

Listener Participation That Works

Good storytelling can reach beyond just engaging the listener's imagination and can engage their voices and bodies as well. Through participation, the storyteller invites listeners into creating something larger than themselves, something that no single listener or the storyteller could create alone. I can say that a million needles of ice are ringing out, but I alone cannot create the experience of sound actually jingling all around us the way that a couple of hundred congregants can if I ask them to take out their keys and shake them. That is the power of listener participation in storytelling. By inviting the listeners to participate in the telling of the story, all become, to some degree, the tellers of the story. All live it on a deeper level.

Inviting congregants into an experience larger than they themselves can create is the basis for any communal worship experience. We could all go home to a corner or atop a mountain to pray or meditate by ourselves. Many of us do on a regular basis and are nourished by such practice. But we come together to worship because there is something we experience through communal worship that we cannot find alone. When we sing together, pray together, listen together, witness one another's joys and sorrows, we have a shared experience. We recognize our interconnectedness with one another and the holy, however we understand it.

Telling a story in a way that allows those present to participate can heighten that feeling of shared experience. It isn't just the sounds the congregation makes together, nor is it just the dramatic effect. It is the act of participating with others to create something that brings a feeling of closeness to those sharing the experience. Such an experience can feel magical, perfect for storytelling.

Listener participation can be a powerful way to engage a congregation in a story, but it is not always the best approach. Some stories are perfect for involving the congregation, but others do not open themselves easily to it. Some may require a delicacy of emotional tone that is best left to the teller alone. Not all plots include elements that easily translate to meaningful participation, or the elements most easily acted out are not pieces of the story the congregation should portray. The emotions and actions acted out have the power to shape the emotional tone, not only of the story but also of those living the story. Be wary of having the listeners act out negative elements of the story as those emotions will likely stick with them. Additionally, adding listener participation may sometimes stretch the time needed to tell the story. Or the space may be limited. Most importantly, storytellers must always consider the artistic merits of whether and how to involve the listeners: Will doing so enhance the experience of the story or not?

Opportunity for Multigenerational Play

When the congregation takes a role in storytelling, it is often playful. Being silly together in a safe environment can work wonders to develop intimacy within a group. If that playfulness simultaneously speaks somehow to our deeper purpose in life, it can generate strong positive feelings. Most storytelling in worship settings is multigenerational. When adults know that the silliness they are being asked to join is a way to pass on our values to our children, they are more than happy to oblige—they are delighted to do so.

Teaching children to participate in the elements of worship geared toward adults can bring many gifts. Children can benefit from learning to be quiet and sit during mediation and prayer, for example. Participating in a story, however, brings children an immediately engaging worship experience. When the adults are willing to participate along with the children, everyone shares a wonderful moment of collective play. A story that introduces a religious or ethical theme helps everyone reflect on deeper values as well.

Listener participation is also an effective way to involve children in co-creating worship. Because they are still developing, young bodies and voices need to be active. Having a role in a story in which they can speak or move allows children to use some of the energy they build up when they are passive for too long.

One might think that teens are generally too aloof or self-conscious to participate in stories directed toward younger children. And indeed, if teens perceive they are being treated like children, they might resist participating. It is possible, though, to respect the developmental maturity of youth while simultaneously inviting playfulness. When among peers with whom they feel comfortable being playful, teens can be especially enthusiastic participants.

Ways to Involve Listeners

Once you have decided that listener participation fits with a particular story you are planning to tell, look for different ways to involve listeners. Give yourself permission to look for the obvious as well as more creative opportunities to involve the audience.

Voice

One of the easiest ways to involve listeners in storytelling is to give the audience a speaking role. Usually this involves a word, phrase, or sound that the congregation speaks when cued. It can be the sound of a particular animal or the repeated answer to a key question. In any story you are telling, look for opportunities to give easy-to-remember and oft-repeated lines to the congregation to speak. This technique is especially effective if the words or sounds initiate some action, magic, or change in the plot. This gives listeners the power to shift the story through their participation.

In "The Sun Goddess of the Heavens," the sound of the roosters raises Amaterasu's curiosity and begins to draw her out of the cave. By giving the role of the rooster to the congregation, we are also giving the congregation the power to shift the story. This power is symbolic, but children, youth, and adults all generally enjoy exercising influence in the world, even if symbolic.

Bodies/Movement

Young children tend to be kinesthetic and full of energy. When children are allowed to incorporate their bodies into the story, they bring a whole new dimension of engagement. Children, youth, and adults can be given motions to perform along with their spoken lines. If you ask them to make the sound of an animal, invite them to make a corresponding movement. This often brings a silly element to the story, so make sure that the action fits the emotional and aesthetic tone of the story you are telling. When telling "The Sun Goddess," I invite the congregation to embody the roosters. I model bending my arms into the shape of wings and bringing my chin forward and back while ko-ko-ko-ko-ro-ing as a rooster does. Most of the congregation will follow suit from the visual cue and become the roosters in body and voice.

Music and Song

Not all stories involve musical elements, but those that do present a natural way to involve listeners. A congregation can be taught a simple song or given a basic rhythm to follow with musical instruments. The musical elements can be embedded within the story. Alternatively, songs or hymns may serve as musical interludes between scenes from a story or drama. *Story, Song and Spirit* by Erika Hewitt offers several examples of services that incorporate story and music into one cohesive whole.

I had the delightful experience of being in a worship service in which Rev. Lauren Smith retold "Snake Alley Band" by Patricia Nygaard. It is the story of a small snake who one day finds himself separated from his band of music-making snakes and learns to enjoy the music of other creatures despite his initial misgivings. What made Smith's retelling so magical was that she led hundreds of us in that service in the rhythmic voicing of the hissing, tail-thumping snakes and then each of the other music-making creatures. The rhythms and sounds were simple and catchy, and the mostly adult attendees readily participated. The story came alive through the music in a way it could not on the page, even as a picture book. It was a wonderful experience that would not have been the same without all of our voices together.

Volunteers

When preparing to tell a story, look for ways to use volunteers from the audience. If your story requires props, consider asking one or two volunteers to help you hold or use them. Look for opportunities to ask children or youth to volunteer to engage them more deeply. Be prepared for children and youth being self-conscious or shy, especially in front of a mostly adult community. For those not confident enough to volunteer, watching other kids play a role in storytelling may be a vicarious thrill. And adults are delighted to see young people participate in worship in even the smallest ways. If you do not get any children or youth willing to come up, be ready to ask for adults—who are perhaps children at heart—to volunteer. Or go on without volunteers.

Successfully Inviting Participation

For some, the idea of telling a story that depends to some degree on getting others to participate is intimidating. "What if nobody plays along?" we may wonder. Some of us may worry that others will think what we are asking of them is dumb, that we will look foolish, and the story will flop. We may fear a tough crowd.

Consider these reassurances. First, those that attend religious services are often invested in perceiving themselves as kind, compassionate people. If you have asked them to help with a story and to participate in a way that is relatively safe and does not compromise their dignity, you will find them eager to please. Considering that many worship elements are dry and passive, participating in a story will often be received with enthusiasm and for some, with plain relief. You are taking a risk by asking others to participate in the story, but it is a rather small risk. The payoff, however, of having an enlivened, joyful shared experience is huge. Even if the story does not go exactly as you hope, don't worry—people don't tend to carry rotten tomatoes to religious services.

Offer a Genuine Invitation

As a visitor at another congregation during a summer service, I watched a professional worship leader invite the only two children present to come forward for the children's time. They declined with a quick shake of the head. At another time of year, a larger group would likely have come forward without hesitation, but not this day. The worship leader pressed the children to participate. The children again declined, appearing more uncomfortable. He waited a moment longer, while the children did not move. Appearing a little embarrassed, the worship leader went on awkwardly, with the children remaining in the pews. Had he been truly okay with "no" at the beginning, or had he been aware of the potential for one or two children to feel singled out, the interaction could have gone differently.

The mere idea of trying to force someone to participate in a story for all ages is absurd. However, when we feel anxious about whether anyone will participate, or we feel that a lack of participation is a statement about our skills as a worship leader or storyteller, then sometimes we find ourselves cajoling others into participation. If we aren't truly comfortable with children or adults declining, however, it isn't a genuine invitation. It is a demand. The invitation is most effective when we anticipate people will want to participate but are able to accept that they may not. We don't want to manipulate people into participating.

Invite Relaxed Participation

How we invite participation significantly affects whether listeners want to participate. More important than any other factor is to invite participation in a nonanxious way. We may be nervous about our own performance telling a story (I usually am to some degree). However, we don't need to be anxious about whether others will participate. If they don't, go on with the story anyway.

Invite participation in a relaxed way. Your sense of humor and fun will be contagious. Keep a sense of humility and, respecting the choice of children, teens, and adults to participate or not, enjoy your storytelling experience.

Sometimes the anxiety about inviting audience participation reflects a fear that there will be too much participation—that it will not end or will become too raucous. You can relieve this anxiety by planning how to cue the participants to start and stop. Then teach them the cues before you start the story or before they begin participating.

Get Participants on Board Beforehand

If your story truly depends upon participation, recruit a few people to be back-ups if no one volunteers. Tip off your friends in the congregation that there will be audience participation elements and ask them to join in. To feel more confident, rehearse the story with them so you know at least a few people will do exactly what you expect or need; they will model it for the other listeners.

Using Props, Costumes, Instruments, and Other Materials

All you actually need to involve listeners in your telling are their voices and bodies. However, using props or materials is a good way to bring the story more fully into the room and involve others in the telling. If your story includes a musical element, consider bringing in musical instruments. Many religious education directors have a supply of simple instruments such as tambourines, bells, and maracas. Recruit children beforehand as volunteers to pass out and later collect the instruments— they'll enjoy helping.

Props impart excitement and interest to your story and provide an opportunity to invite volunteers to help hold or manipulate them. If you want to bring a playful air to your storytelling, try using larger-than-life props. If the story calls for a magic wand, create one from a broomstick and a giant star made from poster board. If a flower appears in the story, make one that is twice the size of your head from sheets of tissue paper. Larger-than-life props are easy to see and appreciate, even in a large crowded room.

You can integrate props into serious stories, if done carefully and artistically. I once retold Jane Yolen's "Owl Moon" for our nighttime Christmas Eve service. A congregant had access to a real stuffed owl from a natural history display. We placed the congregant strategically in the balcony, along with the owl, where she voiced the owl calls from her largely invisible position. At the point in the story when the owl appears, she shined a powerful light on it, providing a surprise for the audience, which fit the story's gently suspenseful tone.

Simple costumes can be brought into a story. Volunteers can be asked to play a character by donning the costume and being directed to pantomime simple actions or to speak simple words. Anything even remotely complex requires a rehearsal. (See chapter 6, on page 133, which describes using drama in worship.) However, simple symbolic actions can be orchestrated by the narrator and incorporated on the fly by volunteers.

But when deciding to use props, costumes, instruments, or other materials, you must consider whether they and the use of participants fit the story, your artistic choices about the story's presentation, and the story's overall emotional tenor. Look for opportunities for creative participation and use of materials that will deepen the story rather than distract from it.

Telling "The Sun Goddess of the Heavens" with Listener Participation

I once told "The Sun Goddess of the Heavens" in a worship service with two hundred plus worshippers at each of two services. I had a horn section that was slated to play that day. I also had an artist in the congregation who had coincidentally made a human-sized sun mask and costume and was willing to pantomime the role of Amaterasu Omikami. I made a six-foot-tall foam-core "mirror." I also had baskets of musical instruments. It was a blast.

I have also told this story in a small congregation with about forty children and adults present. I had no giant mask and costume, no easy way to transport the six-foot foam-core mirror, and no horn section. I did have a couple of baskets of instruments and a bag full of homemade shakers. It was also a blast.

In order to involve your congregation in the telling of this story, all you really need is their engagement. If you can procure a mask, a giant mirror, a horn section, or other musicians or props, then great! By using your imagination and being thoughtful about ways you can involve your listeners, you will find that this story, like many others, holds opportunities for the listeners to be involved in the telling. As always, do what you believe will work best in your setting with the resources you have. And have fun!

As you read through this example of how to involve listeners, feel free to apply similar ideas to other stories you might tell in worship. Start looking for ways that elements like giant mirrors, musical instruments, animal calls, and conga lines could appear in a number of different stories. Think about how you might proactively and effectively invite and direct listener participation so that all of your multigenerational services are just as engaging and fun.

Materials

Minimally, you need the voices of those present and their willingness to engage. The congregation can participate in the telling by using just their voices and bodies. You might consider making or procuring the following resources as well.

Musical Instruments

Simple musical instruments can be used by the congregation to make the music that draws out the Sun Goddess from the cave. Making small shakers is an easy and inexpensive way to provide musical instruments that the children (or adults!) can keep. Plastic eggs can be partially filled with small candies to make shakers, and the children can take them home to eat afterwards. Or collect them at the end of the story so that you can use them again whenever inexpensive and plentiful musical instruments are needed for a storytelling.

The musicians playing that day will likely want to participate in this fun story. If you let them know beforehand, they can be ready to lay down a fun conga beat at the appointed time. Even a pianist alone can add a big sound that will help drive the beat. If you happen to have a horn line, what fun! Whenever you are telling a story, remember to consider how you might use the staff and volunteers as resources.

Large Mirror

I made a six-foot mirror by taping together two pieces of foam core to make one large surface. I cut the foam core in the shape of an elongated octagon, because the myth from the *Kojiki* specifies an eight-sided mirror. I used spray adhesive to affix a layer of aluminum foil to make the surface reflective. I then cut strips of red tag board to make a border. Alternately, you could use an inexpensive, lightweight full-length mirror. Foam core or tag board can easily be made into large two-dimensional props for any story.

Sun Mask/Costume

Creating a sun mask for use in the story could be an enjoyable project for children or youth. They could construct a large papier-mâché mask and paint it bright yellow, orange, and red. The mask will help create an otherworldly feel to the character. A simple costume of similarly colored material worn like a poncho would complete the costume. A volunteer could pantomime the role of Amaterasu as the teller told the tale. Making masks and simple costumes could be effective with any number of stories.

Inviting Participation

In order to help the listeners anticipate their role in the telling as well as to make sure everyone knows what to do, I invite the congregation to help me tell the story before we begin. I give instructions about what they are going to do and tell them what their cues will be to both start and stop. I try not to give away the whole story in this explanation, just the actual words or actions I am asking them to do. Their curiosity about why I would ask them to do such things will create interest and engagement early on in the telling.

Thus, I might introduce the story and their participation in this way:

Today, we are going to tell a story from the most ancient book of Japan, the Kojiki. *This book is a collection of myths similar to the stories of the gods and goddesses of ancient Greece and Rome. Today's story is about the Sun Goddess, Amaterasu Omikami, an important symbol in Japanese culture.*

I say "we" are going to tell a story because I need your help to tell it. Will you help me?

First, I am going to need you to play the part of some roosters. Now, roosters in Japan don't say cock-a-doodle-doo. They speak Japanese, of course, not English, so they use the Japanese phrase "ko-ko-ko-ko-ro." When I give this signal [rooster wings flapping], *then everyone say "ko-ko-ko-ko-ro!" Let's practice.*

Next, we are going to need to sound like we are having a great party with music, so I have some musical instruments that we can use. [ask for assistants to help pass out the musical instruments and collect them after the story is finished]

When I give this signal [point dramatically to the congregation], *we are going to make music just like we are having a grand party. And when I give this signal* [wave arms like conductor stopping an orchestra], *the music will stop. Ready?* [cue musicians; as the congregation plays, feel free to play along yourself with a little conga dance step; cue end] *Now, I will need you to hold your instruments very quietly until I give you the cue, or we will ruin the surprise.*

Finally, I need two volunteers to help hold our very large mirror. I will have you hold the mirror over to the side here until we are ready. When I give you the cue, please bring it forward.

Are we ready? Wonderful! Remember, quiet instruments. We want it to be a surprise.

This script is only one way to introduce this story. You can tell the story without props and still involve the congregation. They can simply use their voices to be roosters and to make music. Lead the congregation in the "Dah, dah, dah, dah, dah, DAH!" of a conga beat. You can encourage them to dance in place and generally whoop it up.

If you do have musical instruments or noisemakers and are concerned that the children will have a hard time holding them quiet (or that their parents will), you may wait until the middle of the story to give instructions. At the point in the story when the gods and goddesses meet to make a plan, you can instruct the congregation on their role. You can lead them in practicing to be roosters and in starting and stopping the music. When they are ready to work the plan, begin the story again. If you have confidence that the children will be able to hold the instruments quietly, build the anticipation early and let the story flow without the break for instructions. You know your congregation and culture and are the best judge of which timing will work best.

Directing Listener Participation

Along with the text of the story, included below are directions written within brackets for cuing and directing listener participation. Because this story lends itself particularly well to physical embodiment, also included are notes for movement that the narrator can use. As with all storytelling, attention to tempo, volume dynamics, and emotional expression will enhance the telling of the story.

Long, long ago, high in the heavens above Japan, was the land of the gods and goddesses.

It was a peaceful land, ruled by the Sun Goddess, Amaterasu Omikami. Amaterasu was a kind and gentle ruler. When she smiled her gentle smile, all the heavens were at peace. [tilt your head to the side and smile serenely]

The Sun Goddess had a little brother named Susano no Mikoto. One day, Susano called up to the heavens, [hold both hands up around mouth, as if calling out] *"Please, sister, can I come and live up in the heavens with all the gods and goddesses?"*

Amaterasu said to her little brother, "If you are to live in the land of the heavens, you must promise to behave and not make any mischief."

"Yes, sister. I promise to behave and not make any mischief." The Sun Goddess smiled her gentle smile, and her little brother climbed up to the land of the gods and goddesses. [repeat head tilt and serene smile]

Susano was the Sun Goddess's little brother, but he was also a powerful god who liked to play rough and rowdy sometimes. At first, he remembered his promise to his sister, but after a while [slight pause]*, he forgot.*

Soon he was stomping through the land, wrecking the rice fields and destroying the canals that the other gods and goddesses had built. [pantomime giant slow-motion stomping]

But Amaterasu did not worry. *"My little brother is just up to some mischief,"* she said, *as she smiled her gentle smile.* [head tilt and serene smile] *"I am sure he will not cause any more trouble."*

But Susano grew rowdier and rowdier. One day, Amaterasu had gathered the women in the loom house to weave a special cloth for the gods. Suddenly [quickly look side to side to make sure no one is looking], *Susano no Mikoto threw a huge horse's hide onto the loom.* [pantomime throwing the horse hide into the room] *The loom broke, sending splinters in every direction.* [suddenly flinch, as if instinctively avoiding a flying object] *Some of the women were hurt.*

Amaterasu was furious. She could no longer smile her gentle smile. She ran to a cave, hid herself inside, and sealed the cave shut with a large boulder. Without the Sun Goddess, the heavens and earth were plunged into darkness.

The other gods and goddesses rushed to the cave. "Sun Goddess," they called, *"the world has been plunged into darkness. Please come out and smile your gentle smile."* [slight pause as everyone listens for the Sun Goddess's response] *But no sound came from the cave.*

The strongest gods and goddesses tried to move the boulder aside. They pushed and they pulled, [pantomime trying to push and pull the boulder] *but they could not make it budge. They needed another plan.*

First, they built a giant bonfire. Then, they brought all of the roosters from the land. Finally, they brought a very large mirror. [motion the volunteers holding the mirror to come forward] *Now they were ready.* [If you instructed the listeners on their roles before the story began, ask them if they are ready and then begin. If you elected to wait to instruct the listeners, do so now.] *They began to play music and dance.* [cue the music; allow it to play for a few measures and then cue for it to end]

Deep inside the cave, Amaterasu heard music and laughter. "How can there be music and laughter when the world has been plunged into darkness?" she wondered. "What is going on out there?" she called from the cave.

"It is the new Sun Goddess," answered the gods. *"We are welcoming her."*

"The new Sun Goddess?" wondered Amaterasu. [spoken with a surprised

127

expression] *She pushed the boulder open a crack.* [pantomime pushing the boulder open a few inches]

The roosters saw the crack of light coming out of the cave and thought it was the dawn. "Kokokoko-ro! Kokokoko-ro!" [cue the congregation to join in by flapping wings and jutting chin outward]

Curious, Amaterasu pushed the boulder open a bit farther. When she peeked out of the cave, she saw before her the light of a sun goddess. "Beautiful!" she said, not recognizing herself in the mirror. She stepped out from the cave. [pantomiming Amaterasu pushing aside the boulder, peeking out toward the mirror, and then stepping out fully] *Just as she did, the strongest god rushed forward and closed the cave behind her.* [one hand motioning the boulder shut again]

Everyone cheered and clapped, for the world was no longer plunged into darkness.

"O, Sun Goddess," they all pleaded. "Never plunge us into darkness again." Seeing how much the other gods and goddesses needed her, Amaterasu Omikami forgot her anger and smiled her gentle smile once again. [head tilt and serene smile]

And her little brother, Susano no Mikoto? He was sent back down to earth for a while to think about what he had done.

[smile and make eye contact with listeners as story finishes]

There are innumerable ways to involve listeners in storytelling. What is described here is intended to spark your imagination rather than prescribe a particular approach. I encourage you to apply your own inventiveness to whatever story you are telling. Be creative as you look for symbolic words or actions that your listeners can embody and that enhance the story. When the opportunity to participate in the story is offered nonanxiously and respectfully, and when approached with a spirit of fun, your congregation will have fun with you.

Life Itself

Long ago, the land of the North was filled with wise old Trees. The Trees stood mighty and tall, and their wide leaves stayed green all year long.

Every morning, Life Itself, a fiery orb, rose in the sky. Life Itself smiled upon the Trees, giving them warmth and light. The Trees smiled upon the humans, giving them wood and fruit. The humans smiled upon each other, sharing what they had.

One day, Life Itself was called to the lands of the South, for it was needed there.

Before it left, it spoke: "Do not fret. My friend Darkness will watch over you while I am gone. Remember, Life Itself returns. Life Itself always returns."

With that, Life Itself turned and moved toward the South. Darkness moved in just as it had promised. Though the air got colder, the humans did not worry, at least, not at first.

One being who lived among the humans was Fear. Fear had always been present, whispering, "Be careful of the fire, lest you get burned. Don't let your children stray too far."

Now that Life Itself moved farther south and Darkness was watching the humans more often, Fear began to speak more plainly. "Beware of your neighbor. Watch out for the forest creatures."

And the humans began to listen . . . and worry.

"Where is Life Itself?" they cried. "Why did it leave us alone?"

The Trees, seeing their worry, called out. "Life Itself returns. Life Itself always returns. You must trust."

The Trees saw that the humans were still afraid, so they called out to Darkness.

As Darkness moved among them, their leaves of green turned to yellow, orange, and red. Surrounded by color, the humans forgot their worries and smiled upon one another again.

Fear, however, continued to speak. "It's getting colder. Will there be enough firewood? Surely you will freeze while your neighbor stays warm and toasty."

The humans began to worry again. They began to cut down branch after branch and then even whole trees.

"Wait!" cried the Trees. "You need only ask, and we will cover you."

The Trees called to Darkness again. As Darkness moved among their branches, their leaves began to fall. A warm blanket of yellow, orange, and red covered the land as far as the eye could see.

The Trees spoke: "Life Itself returns. Life Itself always returns. You must trust." The humans, toasty and warm, smiled upon one another once again.

Fear, however, continued to speak louder and louder. "There is not enough fruit for everyone. Take what your family needs before others will."

Soon, human began to fear human. They started to fight over the fruit, taking more than they needed, more than they even wanted, until others had none.

The Trees looked down upon the chaos and hatred. They could not smile. They could only weep.

Big wet tears rolled down their bare branches. In the cold air of Darkness, those tears froze into tiny needles of ice. Thousands of little icicles rang out in the wind of Darkness, filling the cold air with sound.

Far away, Life Itself heard the tinkling of icicles and knew the Trees had been weeping. Life Itself turned toward the North and reached out. Warmth and love filled those Trees, melting the thousands of icicles and leaving in their place lush, green needles of life.

The humans stretched out their hands. As they touched the green needles, they remembered the promise. "Life Itself returns. Life Itself always returns."

Once again, Life Itself smiled upon the Trees, giving them warmth and light. The Trees smiled upon the humans, giving them wood and fruit. The humans smiled upon each other, sharing what they had.

And Fear? Fear was kept to a whisper, as it should be.

—by Kristin Maier

CHAPTER 6

Storytelling by Groups: Drama in Worship

Bringing story into worship can be accomplished with one voice, through traditional storytelling, or with many voices, through drama. If you have a strong vision of how you want to aesthetically and emotionally present a story, traditional storytelling gives you wide latitude to create that experience. A single teller enjoys almost complete control over mood, language, and aesthetic expression. Of course, any performance ultimately occurs in the relational space between the teller and the listener. The magic of story is always an interactive experience and thus, to a degree, artistic control is never complete. Nonetheless, as the single storyteller, you control the presentation of a story.

Telling a story together as a group through drama is a more complex endeavor. Rehearsals must be scheduled, lines learned, movements and actions coordinated, and so on. Shifting from storyteller to director or cast member changes how one engages the art of storytelling. The single storyteller's tremendous control is traded for the alchemy that comes from a shared vision. As multiple actors come together to tell the story, they invariably contribute their own voices, energy, emotions, and insights. From this greater complexity comes the potential for a deeply layered telling and a powerful, enchanting experience for the congregation.

Drama and storytelling are related yet distinct art forms. Both are rooted in the essential form of the narrative, or story, as a vehicle for communication and thought. Both put forth a relatively whole experience for the audience or listeners to experience and then interpret for themselves. And both engage the imagination of the audience/listeners, although somewhat differently.

The action and images of a story, when conveyed by a single storyteller, play out predominantly in the mind and imagination of the listener. The storyteller verbally supplies the images and intimates at their motion and expression, but the whole of the picture occurs in the mind of the listener.

Drama plays out visually to a greater degree in front of the audience. Imagination still comes into play. Disbelief is still suspended. However, the story is more visual. The audience literally sees the story unfold before them. And they see the story unfold between the characters, as multiple actors interact. Understanding the distinct challenges and potential of bringing drama into worship can help us create an experience that is meaningful and life-giving for both the cast and the congregation.

Attending to Process and Performance

Telling a story collectively is truly a privilege. If you usually tell a story alone as a traditional storyteller, having others also responsible for learning the story and carrying a portion of its emotional and artistic weight will be a treat. You will also encounter the challenges of communicating a vision and working together when multiple visions may be at odds.

Developing a dramatic performance for a worship service is different from working in community or commercial theater. As a religious community, how we work and play with one another is as important as any product or performance we create. In religious community, we intentionally attempt to live by our deepest values. When organizing or directing a performance for worship, the true purpose of both the performance and the process must be clear.

A major reason that we would stage a play or story is to provide a richer, more engaging worship experience for our congregation. We want to genuinely move those witnessing it and to help them experience more deeply that which is sacred and good. We hope that their relationship to God, the universe, and/or each other will be deepened and that, in some small way, they will find themselves transformed.

The performance, though, is only part of what we create together through a dramatic production. We also create an experience for the cast and crew while working with one another. The process of creating drama for worship ought to be as spiritually enriching for those participating as the performance is for those watching. And since we put much more time into the preparing than the witnessing, the process of creating the production may be more transformational for the cast and crew than the performance is for the congregation.

However, we can so easily forget the importance of creating a positive process for the participants. Participants can get into conflicts when they differ in understanding what is expected of one another. Because the outcome of the work together is so public, and takes place in a sacred arena, emotions can run high. The director or organizer must keep the first mission front and center: to treat one another in a loving, respectful way as our religious traditions call us to do. We can't allow our concern for the final product or performance to trump the greater purpose of practicing right relationship with one another. This does not prevent the director, cast, and crew from reaching for artistic beauty and eloquence; this is a big part of the fun when done respectfully. Yet, artistic beauty divorced from an ethos of mutual love and support is ultimately ugly and will taint the performance.

The director or organizer sets a tone early on that establishes respect for the gifts that each person brings. Clear expectations from the outset about rehearsal time, learning lines, and level of investment in the practice and performance ensure a positive experience. The director can also model a sense of appreciation for the energy and effort that each person brings, especially when what someone brings differs from what was hoped for. If the play involves children, we must especially model a positive, mutually supportive environment, because we are teaching our children how to work and be with one another.

Choosing a Script

First, choose a script that will further what you are trying to create and nurture through worship. The content of the play should reflect the overall effort to name what is sacred to the religious community and to better understand how we are called to live and be. See chapter 2 on page 23 for more about selecting appropriate content.

There are some specific questions to consider when looking for plays or stories to dramatize as a group. For example, who will be involved in your production? Is this your first venture into theater in worship? Consider the level of commitment and expertise you will require of your participants. Are you looking for a lighthearted script that will be more forgiving for theater novices? Is there already a tradition of theater in worship at your congregation, with a pool of experienced actors ready for a dramatic challenge? Are you working with energetic, enthusiastic youth who would enjoy an active play with lots of movement?

Consider the length of the script that would be appropriate for your worship service and the time commitment of your actors. Will you be working with adults with limited free time for rehearsal? Will you be working with relatively young children? Is your rehearsal time and length already set into a larger religious education schedule?

Look for a script that fits well with the abilities and resources of those who will be involved. Assess your own level of energy, time, and commitment as well. The success of the dramatic production that your group will offer has less to do with how ambitious or elaborate your production is and more with finding a good fit between play and performers.

Choosing a Format

There are a variety of different formats to choose from when looking for a script. Some formats require more preparation on the part of actors, including memorizing substantial lines and attending multiple rehearsals. Others require little or no memorization and can be pulled off with a single rehearsal. Consider the level of investment of your actors and your artistic goals while choosing a format for your production.

Traditional Play

When a play is traditionally staged, actors are assigned roles and memorize their lines from a script. Plays that fit within a worship context are usually short, having one act or a series of short vignettes. Even short plays require multiple rehearsals to allow the director and actors to shape how the lines are expressed; the blocking, or how the actors move on stage; and how the actors relate to one another. The traditional play depends upon each participant committing to rehearsals and to learning lines. When a group of people is able to make this level of commitment, there is a high level of camaraderie, and preparing and performing for the congregation are wonderful experiences.

Skit

A skit is a short play that is generally approached in a more relaxed manner than a traditional play. The actors have speaking roles, but lines are typically shorter and easier to learn. Some skits even allow the actors to improvise. Staging a successful skit requires some rehearsal so participants can learn even simple lines and rudimentary blocking.

Readers' Theater

Readers' theater is a dramatic presentation read aloud from a script. The readers do not need to memorize lines, but they do need to practice. Costumes or props are not needed, and blocking is not necessary, because readers usually just stand or even sit. The cast typically rehearses together to develop the dramatic interaction of their reading. Stage direction for movement can be added, as can costumes or props. Typically, this direction would be kept fairly simple because the actors need to move or manipulate props while reading from a script.

Narrator-Based Drama

In a narrator-based drama, the narrator delivers the majority of spoken lines. The actors' primary role is to visually present the story the narrator is telling. Costumes and props are typically used to enhance the visual nature of the acting. Actors other than the narrator may have some lines to memorize, even important ones, but they are typically short. In some narrator-based drama, the acting is entirely pantomime, or the narrator can prompt the actors' lines. Due to the minimal memorization, this type of production is low risk for the actors and is well suited for involving a wide range of ages. While narrator-based drama could be done without rehearsal, creating a strong visual scene with minimal confusion and maximum visual effect will require at least one rehearsal.

Creating a Shared Vision

Just as we must "live in the story" to prepare to tell it, we must also "live in the story" to prepare to enact it in a play. As the director, you will read the script multiple times, first to enjoy the drama as written and as it plays out naturally in your imagination. Allow yourself to be moved and engaged by the script as it is. Your initial excitement will help drive your growing artistic vision for the play.

As you read through the play additional times, imagine how you will visually make the play come alive for your audience. What do you imagine the characters wearing? What props are they using? Are there props or costumes that you might want to set in motion early in the process? What movement and emotions will the actors show? How will the actors relate to one another? Make notes of your ideas in your script, identifying the most critical moments that will require your closest attention.

After several readings, think about how you might stage the play. First, consider the area you will use as a stage. If you will be performing the play in your congregation's sanctuary, consider the size and shape of the space. Will you need to temporarily move such objects as an altar or pulpit, or will you have to work around them? Can the action of the play move out into the aisles? Might you utilize the balcony? How can you fully inhabit the space and put the congregation in the midst of the action?

For each scene or part of the scene, imagine specifically where it will play out. Make notes or diagrams as you place the characters and visualize how they will move and interact. Consider how most of the congregation can easily view all of the actors. Think about how to place them on the stage so they won't turn their backs to the congregation, and about where props will be placed or kept.

Put all of these elements together to create a vibrant vision for your play or skit. Make sure that your vision feels exciting, true, and meaningful. The cast and crew will not be inspired by your vision unless you are inspired. If you convey a sense that the production will be fun, or beautiful, or moving, they will catch that sense and make it so.

Once you have a rich, fully developed vision for the play, prepare to hold it lightly. As soon as you begin to share this vision, others' interpretations of the story or script will inevitably change and affect it. "My" vision will soon be "our" vision. Remember that actors are not robots programmed by directors but invariably bring their own artistic vision to their role. An effective director encourages the actors' and crew members' engagement in the collective aesthetic vision.

However, you need not give up all authority (or authorship) of that vision. Moments in rehearsals will require decisions to be made. Individual participants may make suggestions that are too far beyond the original artistic vision of the production. The director keeps the whole production focused on a coherent vision. At other times, the director may need to help actors stay focused on their own performances rather than others'. Even when the director must take a strong role, the best experiences and the best performances come about when the cast and crew as a whole share a vision, not when they feel it is foisted upon them.

Pulling It Off: Logistical Tips

If this were a Broadway play or big Hollywood production, a team of producers would be handling all of the logistical concerns. Those putting on a play for a worship service are usually both director and producer. Creating a quality experience for participants and a quality production for the worship service requires thinking ahead about how to organize numerous aspects. Some proactive attention to detail will pay off through effective rehearsals and an overall positive experience for those involved.

Clearly State Your Expectations

Make sure that all your participants know when and where the rehearsals will be. Let them know when you expect them to know their lines. If you are working with children, be sure to get parents' contact information and communicate your expectations to them. You will need their support to make sure children show up on the right days with everything they need.

Assign Roles

Casting in the theater world involves disappointment, and the level of concern for the participants' feelings in a congregation is greater than on Broadway. In most cases, if casting decisions are made kindly and fairly, everyone will handle those decisions maturely. Nonetheless, think about how you will do casting in a congregational context, particularly when assigning roles to children and youth. Children can be very invested in playing particular roles, and they might take either getting or not getting a part personally.

Think through what you know about the demands of the play and about the people who have expressed interest in participating. Will you simply assign parts yourself? Will you function like a collective and discuss who has the desire, time, and personality to take on various parts? Or will you try a hybrid approach? You could schedule a read-through of the script, asking each person to read for multiple characters. The actors will get a feel for the characters, and you will get a feel for the actors. Everyone can write down the parts they would like to play or be willing to play. Armed with this information and your own observations, make your best effort to cast the play with the well-being of the performance and the cast in mind. You can also proactively express your desire at the start to make sure everyone can participate in a meaningful way even if you are unable to accommodate everyone's wishes. Staying grounded in the production's larger purpose will help everyone remember why you are there together.

Get Materials to Participants Early

Actors must have their roles and scripts early enough to learn their lines thoroughly. Do not put them in the position of having to cram to learn their lines and then be tested in a public worship service. Even people supporting the play behind the scenes need to know early on what props and costumes they need to scrounge up. The director should be several steps ahead of the production in order to help all do their parts without added anxiety.

Use Rehearsal Time Well

The cast and crew's time together is always precious and goes by quickly. Working with a group of people is complicated and unpredictable, so as director, prioritize and use rehearsal time to accomplish what is most essential to preparing the performance, because you are likely to run out of time. Rehearsal should be positive and fun, but keep the group focused on the task. The more work put in during rehearsal, the more fun the performance will be.

The amount of rehearsal time depends on the length and complexity of the play, and what you expect of your actors and participants. A short narrator-based drama requiring only symbolic pantomime can typically be blocked out in one brief rehearsal. If the actors have some speaking lines, plan for more time to allow actors to practice them as well. A readers' theater can also be accomplished with a single, productive rehearsal. Of course, additional rehearsals bring greater depth, nuance, and interactive vigor to the reading. If a skit requires actors to speak lines of any length or to remember when they enter, exit, or speak, plan two or three rehearsals. Plays, even short ones, require multiple rehearsals to help the actors learn what they are to do and then practice enough to gain some confidence in doing so. Children may need more time and support than adult participants. Overall, rehearsal always produces a more polished and confident performance, but people's lives are full. Do the best you can with what you have and try to tailor expectations accordingly.

Enlist the Support of Others

You can run yourself ragged if you take on all the tasks yourself. Meanwhile, you lose an opportunity to share ownership with others in the congregation. Are there people you can ask to help with costumes, props, photographing, or videotaping the performances? Expanding your circle of helpers will also expand the circle of those who will be invested in the production and who will make sure to attend the performance.

Maintain a Positive, Supportive Environment

Your first tool in guiding actors is positive feedback and support. A worship community is not the place to wail about not being able to work under "these conditions." Expect some things to go contrary to your hopes and expectations. Keep your sense of humor. Remember that nobody has to be here working on this project. They want to create something beautiful, as do you. Remind your cast—and yourself—that the larger purpose is to practice right relationship with one another and create a worship service that helps everyone know and experience the holy. Modeling a respectful, gracious attitude will help others do so as well.

Make a Plan B for Anything You Can Imagine

Sometimes, your perfect rehearsals will not result in a perfect performance. For example, if you are working with children in a production, anticipate that some of them will catch whatever nasty virus is circulating. Think through how you will deal with an absent actor in any particular role. Anticipate that the children who practiced with such confidence in rehearsal will become shy and say nothing at all during the performance. Accept beforehand that some key prop or costume will disappear moments before the congregation files into the pews. Simply thinking through such problems before they happen will help you to respond calmly and to adjust as well as possible. We can anticipate some problems, but otherwise, the best plan B is to simply relax and allow the show to be what it will be and appreciate the moment.

Pulling It Off: Artistic Tips

When we start off on a venture of bringing drama into worship, we do so with the hope that what we offer has meaning and a touch of beauty. So much work goes into even a short production that we want to do what we can to ensure that the outcome fits our initial artistic vision. Giving attention to that artistic vision at each step along the way will help make an aesthetically rich experience for the audience and participants.

Generate Excitement

Choose a story you think will engage the actors. Make that first reading together an opportunity to appreciate the power and nuance of the work you have chosen. Encouraging the cast to engage with the characters and the emotions of the play early on will help inspire them to learn their part and perform it with energy and passion. From the very beginning, communicate your vision for the production and encourage their engagement with that vision so that it becomes shared.

Put Yourself in the Pew

As objectively as you can, allow yourself to view the production from the position of those who will be watching it. While some directing will need to take place from the stage, the best vantage point is that of the audience. Are actors upstaging one another—moving toward the back of the stage area so their fellow actors have to turn their backs to the audience? Are they standing in front of one another? Are they speaking loudly and clearly? Is there a way to use the space more dynamically? Could the action more fully fill the sanctuary and reach out to the congregation? If you are acting in a role or reading as the narrator, bring in another person who can sit in the pews and give you this kind of feedback.

Apply Good Storytelling Technique

Review the techniques in chapter 3 on page 47. Help your actors employ them as they rehearse their lines and parts. Actors' ability to employ good technique will vary widely based on experience, commitment, age, and natural instincts for acting. Regardless of these factors, you can help everyone to engage deeply with the story and be moved by it, which will improve the performances.

Focus on helping each person act in a clear, comprehensible way that will allow the story to come through. Are they using their naturally powerful voice so they can be heard? Are they using a good tempo, neither dragging nor speaking so quickly they cannot be understood? Are they conveying emotion without overacting? Do they know their lines? Do they know where they are supposed to stand and how they are supposed to move? When all of your actors manage those basic skills, they will convey the story effectively and will provide an engaging, positive experience for the congregation and themselves. That is a major accomplishment and one to be celebrated.

As you observe your actors in rehearsal, look for distracting elements that can be modified or removed. Are there props, costume elements, or pieces of scenery that are more distracting than engaging? Are there actions, movements, or displays of emotions that do not fit the character or that get in the way of the story? Like good storytelling, good acting often requires restraint. Alternately, are there moments in the play that appear too flat? Do certain actors need more expression, larger actions, more dynamic blocking? Look for adjustments that you can make in rehearsal to help what happens on stage fit with the artistic tone and meaning of the story you are enacting. If there are more adjustments to make than time to rehearse, choose to focus on the changes that will have the most impact.

The Day of the Performance

Before the day of the performance, make sure that your cast and crew know when and where to show up. If children are participating, let their parents know when and where their children need to be and what they should bring with them. Reserve a room in your congregation's building where the actors can get ready. Make sure everyone knows when in the service the play will be and where to gather outside the sanctuary if you will not already be inside for the service.

Give away as many jobs as possible for the actual day of the performance so you can oversee everything rather than try to do it all. Have others take pictures and dim or raise the lights, if necessary. Have others line up the props, costumes, and other materials. Consider having someone with a script prepared to feed lines to the actors, if needed. Line up a friend to be a gofer that day.

Expect nerves on the day of the performance and coach your actors to expect them. Bring a bag of hard candy for dry mouths that come with being nervous. Pull your cast together for a brief moment before the performance. Knowing that you are all in this together can help calm nerves and give courage. Take a moment for meditation, prayer, or silence together. Remind them that this is part of a worship service. Perfection is not expected by or for anyone. A respectful effort offered as a gift will be received as a gift by the congregation. Hopefully, our congregations allow us to be human and love us in our humanness. Encourage them to focus on what they have practiced and to enjoy the moment. And try to enjoy it yourself!

Life Itself

Adapted as a narrator-based play for children and adults

Role	Description	Costume/Prop Ideas
Narrator	A heavy reading part best suited for an adult or youth very comfortable reading aloud.	Any colorful cloth or outfit that does not upstage the other characters.
Life Itself	The role of the sun. A major character with just a few lines, but a presence throughout the play.	A simple costume can be made by draping the actor in yellow/orange/red cloth. Yellow face paint could be used, or a mask could be made that covers the upper portion of the face (not blocking the mouth so the lines can be heard) and extending up with rays of the sun.
Darkness	A nonspeaking part that can be played by one or more people. Darkness functions to change the costumes or props of the Trees.	Simple black, flowing cloaks work well. The actor or actors will need to be able to move easily in their costumes as they will be exchanging the costumes/props for the Trees.
Fear	A major character with several lines. Fear begins quietly, grows in volume and intensity, and returns to a quiet presence at the end.	A sparkling, dark green cloak. This differentiates it from Darkness but still provides an otherworldly air.

Tree1 Tree2 Tree3	Major characters with a few lines each. The Trees undergo a few costume/prop changes.	Large painted pieces of tagboard cut in the shape of the crown of a tree that the actors hold. They could begin with bright green leaves, change to red/orange/yellow leaves, change to dark brown bare branches drawn on tagboard, and end by holding actual evergreen boughs. The boughs might be acquired for free from a Christmas tree lot. Alternately, the trees could wear large colored squares of cloth over their shoulders like shawls that Darkness brings them to change into and out of.
Human1 Human2 Human3+ (non-speaking)	Human1 and Human2 are speaking parts. All humans pantomime actions. Multiple non-speaking humans can be cast, depending on space and number of participants.	Simple peasant outfits. Alternately, they could wear simple gray cloth ponchos or simple green tunics fastened with belts.

Introduction

Narrator: This morning, we will be telling you a solstice story, but we will need your help to make the story turn out right. At one point in the story, I will ask you to help call the sun back to the land of the North. We will all do that together by jingling our keys. (Takes keys out and jingles them.) Can you help by jingling your keys? Or perhaps a grown-up with you has keys you can jingle. Wonderful! Now let's all put our keys away so they stay silent until just the right moment in the story—I will tell you when. And for very little hands, maybe grown-ups can hold the keys until we are ready. Now, for the story of Life Itself.

Role	Lines	Stage Direction
Narrator	Long ago, the land of the North was filled with wise old Trees. The Trees stood mighty and tall, and their wide leaves stayed green all year long.	*Life Itself starts from a seated position, rises, and steps forward. Life Itself turns her head and smiles upon the trees. The Trees turn their heads and smile upon the humans, and the humans smile upon one another.*
	Every morning, Life Itself, a fiery orb, rose in the sky. Life Itself smiled upon the Trees, giving them warmth and light. The Trees smiled upon the humans, giving them wood and fruit. The humans smiled upon each other, sharing what they had.	*Life Itself turns away as if hearing a far off call, then turns back to the Trees and humans to speak.*
	One day, Life Itself was called to the lands of the South, for it was needed there. Before it left, it spoke:	
Life Itself	Do not fret. My friend Darkness will watch over you while I am gone.	
	Remember, Life Itself returns. Life Itself always returns.	

Narrator	With that, Life Itself turned and moved toward the South. Darkness moved in just as it had promised. Though the air got colder, the humans did not worry, at least, not at first.	*Life Itself turns away from the Trees and humans and walks very gradually toward the far end of the sanctuary.*
	One being who lived among the humans was Fear. Fear had always been present, whispering.	*Fear rises from a back corner of the stage area to stand close to the humans.*
Fear	Be careful of the fire, lest you get burned. Don't let your children stray too far.	
Narrator	Now that Life Itself moved farther south and Darkness was watching the humans more often, Fear began to speak more plainly.	
Fear	"Beware of your neighbor. Watch out for the forest creatures."	
Narrator	And the humans began to listen . . . and worry.	
Human1	"Where is Life Itself?"	*Humans huddle in fear, even while Trees begin to speak.*
Human2	"Why did it leave us alone?"	

Narrator	The Trees, seeing their worry, called out.	
Tree1	"Life Itself returns."	
Tree2	"Life Itself always returns."	
Tree3	"You must trust."	
Narrator	The Trees saw that the humans were still afraid, so they called out to Darkness.	*Darkness sweeps forward to deliver the new orange/yellow/red costume or props and take away the green.*
	As Darkness moved among them, their leaves of green turned to yellow, orange, and red. Surrounded by color, the humans forgot their worries and smiled upon one another again. Fear, however, continued to speak.	*The humans marvel at the beautiful colors.*
Fear	It's getting colder. Will there be enough firewood? Surely you will freeze while your neighbor stays warm and toasty.	*Fear speaks louder and more boldly.*
Narrator	The humans began to worry again. They began to cut down branch after branch and then even whole trees.	*Humans mime chopping down invisible trees. The Trees look on aghast.*

Tree1	Wait! You need only ask, and we will cover you.
Narrator	The Trees called to Darkness again. As Darkness moved among their branches, their leaves began to fall. A warm blanket of yellow, orange, and red covered the land as far as the eye could see.

Darkness sweeps in and removes the orange/yellow/red cloth or props, perhaps draping them on the stage floor. The Trees now stand bare.

	The Trees spoke:
Tree1	Life Itself returns.
Tree2	Life Itself always returns.
Tree3	You must trust.
Narrator	The humans, toasty and warm, smiled upon one another once again.

Humans smile upon one another. Trees appear relieved.

	Fear, however, continued to speak louder and louder.
Fear	There is not enough fruit for everyone. Take what your family needs before others will.

Fear continues to speak louder and more boldly.

Narrator	Soon, human began to fear human. They started to fight over the fruit, taking more than they needed, more than they even wanted, until others had none.	*Two humans mime tug-of-war over fruit. The "loser" is left empty-handed. Another human mimes gathering fruit into arms and tries to sneak off.*
	The Trees looked down upon the chaos and hatred. They could not smile. They could only weep.	
Narrator	Big wet tears rolled down their bare branches. In the cold air of Darkness, those tears froze into tiny needles of ice. Thousands of little icicles rang out in the wind of Darkness, filling the cold air with sound.	*Narrator takes out keys, holds them high over head, and jingles them. Allow whole congregation to jingle their keys for a moment, so the sanctuary is filled with the sound. Set own keys down and hold up a hand to signal everyone to stop. Then continue with story.*
	Far away, Life Itself heard the tinkling of icicles and knew the Trees had been weeping. Life Itself turned toward the North and reached out.	*Darkness sweeps in delivering cut evergreen branches that the Trees hold out in their arms.*
	Warmth and love filled those Trees, melting the thousands of icicles and leaving in their place lush, green needles of life. The humans stretched out their hands. As they touched the green needles, they remembered the promise.	*The humans reach out to touch the branches.*

Humans	Life Itself returns. Life Itself always returns.
Narrator	Once again, Life Itself smiled upon the Trees, giving them warmth and light. The Trees smiled upon the humans, giving them wood and fruit. The humans smiled upon each other, sharing what they had.
	And Fear? Fear was kept to a whisper, as it should be.
Narrator	The End.

As the children leave the sanctuary, the Trees can leave by different aisles and hold out the evergreen branches for the children and adults of the congregation to touch.

Why the Chimes Rang

Long ago in a faraway land, there was once the most breathtaking church. Every Sunday and every Christmas Eve, people from all over climbed the hill to enter through its magnificent stone archways.

The great room was so long that those inside could hardly see the other end. Its organ was so grand and loud that for miles around the people could feel it rumble like thunder before a storm. And on Christmas Eve when the church was lit up and crowded with people, a more beautiful sight could not be seen.

Most breathtaking of all were the chimes that hung in the enormous bell tower. Some said the bells sounded like angels far up in the sky. Others said the bells sounded like a strange wind singing through the trees. Everyone agreed they were the most beautiful chimes ever heard.

The chimes only rang on Christmas Eve, when people brought offerings to the Holy Child. When the best offering was laid on the altar, the sound of the chimes would ring out from high above in the tower. There were no ropes long enough to ring the bells. Some said the angels rang them. Others said it was the wind.

Sadly, no one had heard them for years and years. Over time, people gave less and less from the heart and had become more and more concerned about what their neighbors gave. Every Christmas Eve, the wealthiest people still crowded to the altar, each one trying to bring some gift more impressive than any other. Each Christmas Eve, the church was still crowded with all sorts of people who hoped they might hear the wonderful bells ring. But though the service was splendid and the offerings plenty, the chimes were silent.

In a little country village miles away a little boy named Pedro lived with his little sister, Luisa. They had heard about the wonderful church and its Christmas Eve service. They had no great gift to offer, but they longed to see the celebration for themselves.

"I have even heard," Pedro said, "that when the grand organ plays and the choir sings, it feels as if the Holy Child is right there." They agreed they must go.

On Christmas Eve Pedro and Luisa walked through the blowing snow, drawing their cloaks against the bitter wind. Just as they were about to enter the city, they saw something in the snow. It was a poor woman who had fallen.

Pedro knelt down to rouse her, but he could not. Neither could they carry her. He looked up at the church on the hill. Sounds of the organ were beginning to rumble. He turned to Luisa.

"I cannot leave her," said Pedro. "You will have to go alone. Everyone has gone to church now, but when you come back, you can bring help. I will keep her warm with my cloak until you return."

"But you'll miss the Christmas service!" cried Luisa.

"You must see and hear everything twice," Pedro told her. "Once for you and once for me. When you return with help, you can tell me all about it."

Luisa reluctantly turned to go. "Here," said Pedro, taking the only copper piece from his pocket. "Lay this on the altar for me, as a gift to the Holy Child." Luisa took the coin and hurried toward the church.

That night, the church had never looked so bright and beautiful. The organ played and the choir sang until the walls shook. When it was time for the offerings, a parade of wealthy men and women marched up to lay down their gifts to the

Holy Child. Some brought exquisite jewels; other brought heavy baskets of gold or great works of art.

Last of all, the king approached the altar. The crowd gasped as he took the royal crown from his head, and laid it gleaming on the altar. Everyone looked up toward the tower, certain the bells would ring now. But the only sound was the ordinary wind.

The choir started the final hymn. Suddenly, the organist stopped playing. The minister held up his hands for silence. Everyone stopped to listen.

There it was, softly at first and then louder and clearer. The notes were sweeter than any they had heard before, rising and falling from so high above. For a moment, everyone just stood and listened. Then they turned to look at the altar.

There a young girl stood, placing a single copper piece atop the pile of riches. And just beyond the city walls, a boy sat in the snow, smiling as he listened to the sound of Christmas chimes in the winter air.

—original text by Raymond MacDonald Alden
adapted for telling by Kristin Maier

CHAPTER 7

Starting a Tradition of Storytelling in Your Congregation

The presence of a single storyteller in a congregation can make a tremendous difference in the quality of worship. Congregants will look forward with anticipation when they know a story will be part of the service. Imagine what worship might be like if storytelling were more than a rare occasion and instead became a regular part of worship, even a tradition in your congregation.

Preparing a story does take effort and time, however. For one person to prepare more than a few stories in any calendar year is a serious commitment. Some individuals have extensive experience or an exceptional gift for learning and telling stories, but those folks are rare. For most congregations, regularly incorporating storytelling in worship is best accomplished as a team effort. If one storyteller can offer two or three stories a year, then a pool of three or four tellers could offer six to twelve a year. A pool of six or eight tellers could offer many more. Since people often travel during holidays, having a pool of storytellers would also increase the chance that a storyteller was available for those important multigenerational holiday services.

Cultivating a team of storytellers in a congregation can be a challenge. Not many people have experience telling stories in front of an audience, and many find the forum too public to explore a new skill. Most religious professionals or seminary students are not trained in storytelling and many staff and members have full schedules already. Creating a tradition of storytelling in our congregations will likely not happen spontaneously. We have to do it intentionally and together.

If you are the only storyteller (or aspiring storyteller) in your congregation, what might happen if you put out the call to others to join you? The value in finding even one kindred spirit would be enormous. If there are already multiple storytellers in your congregation, gathering together could allow you to plan the liturgical year with some intentionality. Even a small community of storytellers could look for more ways to incorporate storytelling in worship and encourage others to join the effort.

Creating a Safe, Supportive Community of Tellers

More than sharing the workload, a community of storytellers can help build energy within a congregation for the art of storytelling. A community of tellers can support one another through sharing story resources, experiences, concerns, triumphs, and a continuing passion and interest in the art form. This camaraderie plants the seeds for inspiring future tellers, as others in the congregation see people they know preparing and telling stories. Instead of hearing, "I could never do that," we might begin to hear, "Maybe I could do that too!"

For someone new to storytelling, venturing into such an activity can be intimidating. Even meeting with a group of others interested in storytelling can feel risky. For a gathering like this to work, it must be a safe, supportive place for people to try new skills and take risks. You can take several concrete steps to intentionally create safety in such a community.

Clarify Your Larger Purposes

Of course, we all love it when our efforts result in a moving or transcendent worship service. This kind of success, however, isn't our deepest purpose. Sometimes, despite our best effort and the best efforts of others, worship does not happen in the way we imagine. When that occurs, we have a different opportunity to live into our larger purpose of accepting one another as whole people or as children of God. We need to hold up this religious value, and to hold ourselves to it in order to create a safe, supportive environment for taking artistic risks in worship. When people take

160

risks in a worship service, we must remember that we are called to love one another and ourselves as we are—human, imperfect, and wonderful. We can build this ethos in our circle of storytellers and also in the wider congregation.

Commit to the Practice of Nonjudging

When we practice nonjudging, we strive to see the whole person before us. This discipline requires us to look beyond the immediate flaw that we notice and hold as much of the whole complex truth as we can. It calls us to move beyond narrow labels of good and bad and to let go of the assumption that we are entitled to bestow those categories on others or their contributions. In a worship context, nonjudging does not preclude having opinions and reactions about what is fitting or not fitting for worship. But it does call us to have a loving response to what happens in worship. A loving, nonjudging environment will go a long way in establishing safe, supportive community for storytelling.

Allow New Tellers to Start Small

To create this environment, we must acknowledge and affirm others' fears or anxieties. We can allow folks to determine how great a risk they are willing to take as a way of honoring their feelings and perceptions about their safety level. Encourage new storytellers or readers to take risks without being pressured to take the stage too early or in ways that feel uncomfortable. This is another way of accepting what each person brings as a gift.

Identify and make available opportunities to those interested in taking relatively small risks. Instead of asking a new teller to take on the most well-attended holiday service, provide opportunities to begin gradually, perhaps with a more intimate or lightly attended service. Connect storytellers with religious education teachers who would welcome them to visit their classroom. Encourage tellers to begin with reading a story in worship to gain confidence for using dramatic skills in front of the congregation.

Allow the Storyteller to Direct and Limit Feedback

Telling a story in a worship service will usually generate plenty of feedback. In a reasonably healthy congregation, most of that feedback will be supportive and encouraging. Feedback from a community of fellow storytellers can carry a different weight. Because fellow storytellers know what goes into the performance of a story, their feedback can be experienced more as judgment, because they understand better the process and possibilities of storytelling.

Unsolicited feedback or advice can be poison to a community of storytellers that is striving to be truly supportive and safe. Standing up and telling a story involves taking a very public risk. Unsolicited advice can hold the underlying message that the teller "didn't do it right." It is important, then, to keep one's critical thoughts to oneself and simply support fellow storytellers. When asked for feedback, offer it without judgment and with appreciation for the gift of the other's effort and talents.

When telling stories in a circle of storytellers, the same guidelines apply. Practicing a story in front of other tellers still makes one vulnerable, especially if the other tellers are more experienced. Tellers must always have the option of receiving no feedback and simply accepting congratulations and support for taking the risk of trying something new. Tellers also need to have the option of asking for limited, specific feedback. It isn't important that you or I can see every little "mistake" in a telling. It is far more important that the teller continues to feel supported as a person in charge of his or her own development.

Starting Up a Storytelling Guild

A storytelling guild ultimately requires only two people willing to participate. Having even one willing partner can make a world of difference for a storyteller hoping to reflect on and develop the art. All of the skill-building exercises can be practiced with a dyad, and having two storytellers in a congregation doubles your capacity for bringing story into worship. If you are in a small congregation or if storytelling is new in your setting, finding even one other teller is an accomplishment to celebrate.

Of course, the more storytellers that participate in a guild, the more energy, support, and insight will be available. Even a half dozen engaged storytellers can bring a critical mass of energy and support and make for lively sessions. Finding that handful of dedicated storytellers, however, might require recruiting far more participants initially. Life tends to intervene and prevents many of us with good intentions from participating.

Cast Your Net Widely
To establish a guild or community of tellers, cast your net widely. Personal invitations are often the most powerful recruiting tool. Do not hesitate to ask those who you think might be interested and who could bring positive energy to the group. However, we can never know who might be waiting for just such an opportunity to get involved. Use a variety of channels to open the invitation to everyone (e.g., email, newsletter, website, weekly bulletin, social media) to get the word out and raise awareness and support for the effort throughout the congregation. If your congregation is small or you are finding a limited response, consider offering your invitation to members of other nearby congregations. Such relationships could lead to future storytelling exchanges between congregations.

Build Energy and Interest
You might consider speaking with the minister, the Worship Committee, and the Religious Education Committee to boost excitement and support for the effort. When you make your pitch, emphasize how storytelling can make multigenerational services more accessible and meaningful for children. Explain that these skills can be used in Children's Chapels and in classrooms. Invite members of the committee to attend your first meeting to learn more. Ask for names of those beyond the committee who might be interested so that you can invite them personally. Ask how you can get the word out to religious education teachers.

In your invitation, be clear that individuals with any level of experience—or none—are welcome and encouraged to attend. Emphasize that the goal of the group is to create a safe, mutually supportive environment to learn to tell stories and develop the skills and enjoyment of storytelling. Point out that participating does not necessarily mean signing up for public telling; participants choose how, when, and if they share stories in your congregations.

Plan Your Initial Gathering

The goal of your first session is to create a shared vision for what this group can be and to establish a tone of mutual respect, support, and overall safety from the very beginning. It is important to be clear about your hopes and expectations, but even more important is seeking to understand the hopes, expectations, and even fears of those who would become participants. Begin with listening. If your group is particularly small, this conversation can be more informal and perhaps include a discussion of how to find others who might want to participate. If it is a larger group, a more structured format will help make sure there is room for everyone's concerns and perspectives. If you are so fortunate as to have a particularly large group, you may need to discuss the logistics of finding adequate spaces to accommodate the noise levels of so many pairs practicing together.

See page 173 for a guide for leading the group through an eight-session workshop. In this workshop series, participants are introduced to one another, learn the skills of storytelling in worship, and practice storytelling in a supportive environment.

Nurture an Ongoing Tradition of Storytelling

Once a tradition of storytelling begins to take root in your congregation, continue to look for ways to nurture that tradition. A living tradition changes and grows and requires some attention to stay healthy. Continue to seek out and nurture new storytellers, even as you give opportunities and support to existing storytellers. Allow for the introduction of new stories or new ways of telling stories, even as you retain favorite stories in the liturgical cycle. A tradition requires a balance of keeping what is familiar and bringing in new people and new material. Most importantly, a healthy tradition is based in a mutually supportive circle that stays grounded in the larger purposes of worship and beloved community.

Prairie Tree

The tree didn't remember the day the family rolled over the prairie and stopped at the bottom of the gentle hills. It didn't watch as they built their home out of sod and bits of lumber.

The tree couldn't have recalled how the family rode out to the stand of bur oaks to collect the furry acorns. It didn't watch them plant the acorns or see them celebrating when one green shoot rose up.

But the tree did remember the family carrying water all the way from the river to pour on the sapling when the prairie sun beat down. It recalled how the children would lie under its circle of shade and giggle and chatter. The tree would chatter back in its own whispering way.

Then one day, the tree saw the family pack up all they owned. It felt the arms of the children circle its slender trunk and watched as they rolled over the hills and out of sight.

After that, no one brought the little tree water when the prairie sun beat down. Some years were so dry, the tree didn't grow taller at all, just twistier and more gnarled the way bur oaks do.

Maybe it was the dryness or maybe it was the ground squirrels and mice that were hungry for its acorns, but no other trees sprouted there. The little bur oak stood alone at the bottom of the gentle hills. It watched the big prairie sky and listened to the chatter of the birds and creatures that came and went. It knew no other family.

Then, one day, two crows came to rest in its branches. They cawed and squawked about their sisters and brothers and cousins the way that crows do.

"Family," the tree whispered aloud. "I once had family."

"Family," said the crows. "Everybody's got family."

"No," said the tree. "They rolled away."

"Rolled away?" squawked the crows. "Your family is just over that hill."

"My family?" asked the tree. "The children?"

"Children!?" squawked the crows even harder. "Your family of *trees* is just over that hill. Can't you see them?"

The tree stretched as far upward as its twisty branches would allow, but it could not see beyond the hills around it.

"No," said the tree. "I cannot."

"What a shame," said the crows, looking the tree up and down. "You're about as tall as a bur oak can get in these parts."

"What a shame. What a shame," said the crows and they flew away.

Once again, the tree stood alone at the bottom of the gentle hills.

"A family of trees," it thought. "A family of trees."

It tried again to stretch as high as its twisty branches would allow, but it was no use. It still could not see above the hills around it.

"I must see them," thought the little tree. "I must."

The little bur oak dug its tap root deeper into the soil. It reached down and down until it felt just a little moisture. It pulled the moisture through its roots, up into its trunk, and all the way to its branches. It spread its leaves wide to catch the prairie sun. Then it stretched and reached, and reached and stretched. It felt as if it was higher in the prairie sky than it had ever been before.

166

Still, it could not see over the hills around it. The tree drooped over right where it stood.

Then, just barely, it heard a whisper. The tree stilled its own branches to listen.

There it was, the whisper of a tree, of *many* trees.

The little bur oak sent its root down a little bit deeper. It spread its leaves a little bit wider, and it reached up just a little bit higher.

Until, just over the hill, it could see the twisty, gnarled tops of bur oak trees swaying under the big prairie sky.

On days when the wind was just right, it could hear those bur oaks whispering away. And on days when the wind was just right, the now not-so-little bur oak could whisper right back and chatter away to its family of trees.

—by Kristin Maier

CHAPTER 8

Storytelling as a Spiritual Journey

I have offered through this book the principles that I believe render a story powerful and engaging, especially in a worship context. I hope that the techniques and methods described help to make the art of storytelling a more accessible, richer experience for those willing to venture into it. You may find that you tell stories much differently than I do. This does not make your way wrong or less effective. For every storyteller living in the world, there is a different and wholly authentic way of telling a story.

As storytellers, we have two true tests of the degree of authenticity we have achieved through our telling. One test is our own experience of the telling and the way that it affects us. The other is the reaction of the audience and the way it affects them. It matters far less which methods and techniques you use to create that experience and far more that they simply work for you as the teller and for your audience.

Our growth as storytellers will come as we honestly assess these two tests to the best of our ability. We must be able to be honest with ourselves, moment to moment, as we work with a story. When we tell any piece of it, we must continually ask if we are telling it in a way that feels true to the story and to our understanding of it. We must continually ask ourselves if there is a way that we can grow as tellers so that our rendering of a story is more true to our vision and that of our audience. Such questioning does not reflect inexperience or incompetence, but the appropriate humility that leads to excellent telling.

When others give us feedback, through their words, their reactions, or their lack thereof, we are left with holding the task of figuring out what part of that

169

feedback we can honestly take in. None of us need ever simply accept another's assessment as the ultimate word. If the feedback is offered in an unsupportive or demeaning way, we need not accept it at all. Any evaluation of someone's art has as much to do with the evaluator as the artist or artwork itself. But another's reaction to our storytelling can be a gift that allows us to see what we are sometimes too close to see ourselves. If we are able to take in their honest reaction in a nonjudgmental way, there is always something to learn either about ourselves, the listener, or both. Often, what others see is a beauty and magic in our storytelling that transcends our performance or technique. If we have fallen under the illusion that our performance should be perfect, seeing the honest beauty and magic of our art through another's eyes is a particularly valuable gift.

Ultimately, we aim not for perfection but for authenticity. Authenticity is fundamental to any relationship of integrity; storytelling is no different. When we allow ourselves to fully enter the story and be naturally and honestly affected by it, then we start to form an authentic relationship with the story itself. When we share those honest reactions to the story through our telling, then we start to form an authentic relationship to the audience.

Being consciously aware of the technique we use in relating the story need not take us away from that fundamental experience of authenticity. Making an intentional decision about how we communicate need not be artifice, but simply an artistic choice that brings our experience of telling the story closer to our experience of living the story. If our artistic choices bring our audience into a deeper relationship with the story, its characters, and the themes it explores, then we are also helping them live the story more authentically and deeply.

Tapping that authentic reaction during the performance of a story requires a tremendous amount of practice. Repetition need not make that reaction to the story less authentic. Rather, it can help us reliably find the path to that genuine reaction in the moment of performance. By entering the same story again and again, we develop a deeper relationship to that story, to our audience, and even to ourselves. There is an additional, less tangible, side effect to that kind of repetition. In reaching for storytelling as art, we must reach past our own likes or dislikes. We must forget ourselves and our personal desires in order to put our attention on the story and choose what is best for the story and our audience. We forget ourselves, for at least a moment, in service of the greater good.

As much as authenticity and honesty are essential to the art of storytelling, so is joy. Good, hard work for our art should not be joyless. When any of us finds joy in telling a story, whatever our inevitable limitations may be, that joy will shine through and carry the story in a way that even the most perfect technique could not. Our love of the art form and our love of the stories we choose to tell will bring something to storytelling that reaches beyond instruction.

That quest for authenticity, self-honesty, and joy takes us into a realm where art and spirituality intersect. Engaging storytelling as an art rather than just a teaching tool can be a spiritual practice and journey all its own. In *The Way of the Storyteller*, the great storyteller Ruth Sawyer writes that at heart, storytelling is a spiritual endeavor:

> It is a call to go questing, an urge to follow the way of the storyteller . . .
> that each might find "something for which his soul had cried out." I believe
> it to be something that transcends method, technique—the hows and the
> whys. It is, in the main, spiritual experience which makes storytellers.

Like any spiritual journey, the art of storytelling will call us to stretch and grow. Depending on how deeply you engage the art and your own growing edges, you may find yourself stretching beyond what you initially thought yourself capable of. That is not always comfortable—but what authentic spiritual journey is? The joy and meaning that I have experienced through the art of storytelling have been well worth any effort involved. I wish you the very best on your own journey with storytelling, wherever it might take you. I hope you find along the way the kind of joy and meaning I have come to cherish.

Storytelling Workshop Series

Session One: Introduction (50–60 minutes)

Introductions (5–10 minutes)

Ask all participants to introduce themselves. You might have them to share their answers to the following questions. Use a whiteboard or large paper tablet to record their responses.

> What drew you to this group?
> What do you hope to get out of this group?
> What fears, if any, do you have about this group or storytelling in general?
> Have you told stories before?

Purpose/Vision (10–15 minutes)

This is your chance to articulate your vision as the organizer(s). State it clearly and succinctly.

Open a discussion about how your vision as organizer(s) fits with the articulated hopes and fears of the participants. Identify and record the shared vision that arises from this discussion. If there are significant differences among the visions of the participants, your group might need to talk openly about how or if everyone's needs can be met through this group.

Ground Rules (10 minutes)

In order for the group to provide a reasonably safe environment for learning new skills and taking risks, all members of the group should agree on the ground rules.

You may want to present a set of suggested ground rules. The group should have an opportunity to discuss them, modify any that seem unclear or problematic, and add any they feel are missing. Alternately, you can facilitate building a set of ground rules from scratch. Either way, all members of the group should agree to one set. If significant differences arise, the participants may be envisioning two distinct kinds of groups. In this case, you may need to revisit the purpose and vision.

Schedule and Overall Format (10 minutes)

Initiate a discussion about how often your group will meet. The sample sessions included here consist of five hour-long skill-building sessions, followed by two different formats for sharing prepared stories.

Your group could choose to move through the skill-building sessions more quickly by combining two sessions into a longer, hour-and-a-half meeting. Or, depending on the experience level of participants, your group could move through some skills more quickly or skip directly to the formats for sharing prepared stories. Design a format that fits the needs and desires of your participants.

If the group has a broad range of experience and skill levels, consider asking the more experienced storytellers to lead the demonstration and explanation portions of the skill-building sessions. Or ask them to tell the warm-up stories suggested for the beginning of the sessions called "Telling to a Supportive Peer" and "Telling to a Supportive Audience."

Building Enthusiasm (15 minutes)

Make sure to bring some of the fun of storytelling into this first session. Prepare to tell a story, or arrange beforehand to have an experienced teller in the group share one. Set the tone for the sessions with this first story and make the telling an exercise in appreciation rather than an opportunity for critique. It should be offered and received as a gift. Or bring in one of your favorite picture books to read to the group. You could also bring a video or audio recording of a skilled and experienced storyteller so that you may listen and enjoy together.

Do your best to end on time and express gratitude for those who took time out of their personal lives to attend. Each person's presence is a gift. Modeling a positive, respectful demeanor will keep the group upbeat and will help retain participants.

Session Two: Skill Building: Dynamic Volume (approx. 60 minutes)

Before You Meet

Ask participants to bring a story to the session. They can bring a picture book, folktale, myth, or story of their own. The story should be relatively short and appropriate to share in your congregation. It does not have to be memorized and it does not need to be elaborate. Participants will use this story to practice storytelling technique.

Prepare a brief explanation and demonstration on using a naturally powerful and dynamic voice. See chapter 3 on page 47.

Gathering (5–10 minutes)

So often, we rush into whatever activity or meeting we are attending without taking time to mentally transition to the new space we are in. Spending only a few minutes to help a group become present in the moment at hand will shape every moment thereafter.

Ground your group in your religious setting. Remind everyone that you are no longer at work, the grocery store, or a sporting event. You are together as a religious community. Light a chalice (a Unitarian Universalist tradition), light a candle, take a few minutes for silent meditation, pray together, read scripture, or read a poem. Do something symbolic that helps participants remember where they are and who they are in that space.

Remind each other of the purpose and vision of this group and the ground rules you agreed upon. This reminder shouldn't be lengthy or preachy, but in the first few meetings, everyone will need help remembering the specifics of your agreement.If the group does not know each other well, ask participants to introduce themselves and perhaps name one of their all-time favorite stories.

Using Our Naturally Powerful and Dynamic Voices

Demonstration (10 minutes)

Offer a demonstration, based on chapter 3, of how to use one's naturally powerful voice and how to use a dynamic voice that fits with the content of a story.

Practicing Together (20–25 minutes)

Ask the group to divide into pairs. Participants will use the story they brought to practice these skills.

Instructions to Participants

Provide the following instructions to the participants:

Read aloud to your partner all or a portion of the story you brought.
1. Begin reading with what feels like a natural volume.
2. Try reading it with half the volume.
3. Try reading with a much louder voice.
4. Look for places where the story might warrant an increase or decrease in your base volume.
5. Reflect on these questions with your partner:
   - How did changing the volume change your experience of the story?
   - How did it change your comfort level as a speaker?
   - Is there a level at which you felt more comfortable or familiar as a speaker?
   - What volume do you imagine would be most comfortable to a listener?
6. Invite feedback from your partner.
7. Switch roles.

Sharing (10–15 minutes)

Ask for one or two volunteers who are willing to read their story to the entire group. Emphasize that this is an opportunity for appreciation rather than critique. In keeping with the ground rules, no feedback should be given except that which is invited. Focus instead on appreciating the story and the reader's willingness to share.

Closing (10 minutes)

Ask for feedback about the session. Thank everyone for coming. Extinguish the candle or chalice. Clarify when you will have your next meeting and what the participants should bring or prepare.

Session Three: Skill Building: Elastic Tempo (approx. 60 minutes)

Before You Meet

Ask participants to bring a story to the session. They can bring a picture book, folktale, myth, or story of their own. The story should be relatively short and appropriate to share in your congregation. It does not have to be memorized and it does not need to be elaborate. Participants will use this story to practice storytelling technique.

Prepare a brief explanation and demonstration on establishing a good base tempo and using an elastic tempo. See chapter 3 on page 47.

Gathering (5–10 minutes)

Help your group mentally transition and become present in the moment at hand. Light a chalice, light a candle, offer a prayer or reading. Remind each other of the purpose and vision of the group and the ground rules you agreed upon. If the group does not know each other well, ask participants to introduce themselves and perhaps the story they brought.

Establishing a Base Tempo and Using an Elastic Tempo

Demonstration (10–15 minutes)

Offer a brief explanation and demonstration, based on chapter 3, of how to establish a good base tempo and how to use an elastic tempo, including the dramatic pause.

Practicing Together (20–25 minutes)

Ask the group to divide into pairs. Participants will use the story they brought to practice these skills.

Instructions to Participants

Provide the following instructions to the participants:

Read aloud to your partner all or a portion of the story you brought.
1. Begin reading with what feels like a natural tempo.
2. Try reading it more slowly and more deliberately.
3. Try reading it more quickly.
4. Look for places where the story might warrant an increase or decrease in your base tempo. Practice reading the story while speeding up or stretching out the tempo to fit what is happening in the narrative. Where there is an opportunity, try inserting a dramatic pause.
5. Reflect on these questions with your partner.
   - How did changing the base tempo affect your experience of telling the story? How did it affect your experience of hearing the story? Does a faster or slower tempo feel more natural to you? Did one base tempo fit that particular story better than another?
   - How did using an elastic tempo change your experience of telling the story? Did it feel effective as you heard yourself read it?
   - Did it feel natural or unnatural as a teller to slow down and speed up within a story?
   - Was there an opportunity for a dramatic pause? How did it work?

6. Invite feedback from your partner.
7. Switch roles.

Sharing (10–15 minutes)

Ask for one or two volunteers who are willing to read the story they brought to the entire group this time. Emphasize that this is an opportunity for appreciation rather than critique. In keeping with the ground rules, no feedback should be given except that which is invited. Focus instead on appreciating the story and the reader's willingness to share.

Closing (10 minutes)

Ask for feedback about the session. Thank everyone for coming. Extinguish the candle or chalice. Clarify when you will have your next meeting and what the participants should bring or prepare.

Session Four: Skill Building: Using Movement (approx. 60 minutes)

Before You Meet

Ask participants to bring a story to the session.

Prepare a brief explanation and demonstration on using movement to enhance a story. See chapter 3 on page 47.

Gathering (5 minutes)

Help your group mentally transition and become present in the moment at hand. Light a chalice, light a candle, offer a prayer or reading. Remind each other of the purpose and vision of the group and the ground rules you agreed upon. If you have newcomers to the group, make sure to do introductions again.

Using Movement to Enhance the Story

Demonstration (10–15 minutes)

Offer a brief explanation and demonstration, based on chapter 3, on how to use movement to enhance a story.

Practicing Together (20–25 minutes)

Ask the group to divide into pairs. Participants will use the story they brought to practice these skills.

Instructions to Participants

Provide the following instructions to the participants:

1. Read through your story and look for places you might add movement. Spend a few minutes trying out different movements until you find what seems to fit.
2. Read the story to your partner using the movements you have explored.
3. Invite feedback of your choosing, or simply ask for appreciation or affirmation.
4. Reflect with your partner on the experience of using movement in telling the story. What felt natural, unnatural, fitting to the story, or potentially distracting?
5. Switch roles.

Sharing (10–15 minutes)

Ask for one or two volunteers who are willing to read their story to the entire group. Emphasize that this is an opportunity for appreciation rather than critique. In keeping with the ground rules, no feedback should be given except that which is invited. Focus instead on appreciating the story and willingness to share.

Closing (10 minutes)

Ask for feedback about the session. Thank everyone for coming. Extinguish the candle or chalice. Clarify when you will have your next meeting and what the participants should bring or prepare.

Session Five: Skill Building: Developing Characters (approx. 60 minutes)

Before You Meet

Ask participants to bring a story to the session.

Prepare a brief explanation and demonstration on developing characters in a story. See chapter 3 on page 47.

Gathering (5–10 minutes)

Help your group mentally transition and become present in the moment at hand. Light a chalice, light a candle, offer a prayer or reading. Remind each other of the purpose and vision of the group and the ground rules you agreed on. If you have newcomers to the group, make sure to do introductions again.

Developing Characters

Demonstration (10–15 minutes)

Offer a brief explanation and demonstration, based on chapter 3, on how to develop characters in a story.

Practicing Together (20–25 minutes)

Ask the group to divide into pairs. Participants will each use the story they brought to practice these skills.

Instructions to Participants

Provide the following instructions to the participants:

1. Read through the story looking for ways you might represent the characters. Is there a small change in voice, posture, tempo, or volume that can communicate those shifts in character in a way that enhances the story?
2. Practice these characterizations as you read or tell the story to your partner.
3. Reflect on the experience with your partner. Did certain changes in characterization seem more fitting than others? Were some harder for you to convincingly portray? Were some easier? What effect did these character changes have on the story?
4. Invite feedback of your choosing, or simply ask for appreciation or affirmation.
5. Switch roles.

Sharing (10–15 minutes)

Ask for one or two volunteers who are willing to read their story to the entire group. Emphasize that this is an opportunity for appreciation rather than critique. In keeping with the ground rules, no feedback should be given except that which is invited. Focus instead on appreciating the story and willingness to share.

Closing (10 minutes)

Ask for feedback about the session. Thank everyone for coming. Extinguish the candle or chalice. Clarify when you will have your next meeting and what the participants should bring or prepare.

Session Six: Skill Building: Communicating and Inviting Emotion
(approx. 60 minutes)

Before You Meet

Ask participants to bring a story to the session.

Prepare a brief explanation and demonstration on communicating and inviting emotion as a storyteller. See chapter 3 on page 47.

Gathering (5 minutes)

Help your group mentally transition and become present in the moment at hand. Light a chalice, light a candle, offer a prayer or reading. Remind each other of the purpose and vision of the group and the ground rules you agreed upon. If you have newcomers to the group make sure to do introductions again.

Communicating and Inviting Emotion as a Storyteller

Demonstration (10–15 minutes)

Offer a brief explanation and demonstration, based on chapter 3, on how to communicate and invite emotion as a storyteller.

Practicing Together (20–25 minutes)

Ask the group to break into pairs. Participants will each use the story they brought to practice these skills.

Instructions to Participants

Provide the following instructions to the participants:

1. Choose a section of your story. Read through it on your own first, feeling for a level of emotion that opens the door for the listener's own emotions without overwhelming them.

2. Experiment with different levels of expression. Try varying your tempo, volume, pitch, facial expression, movement, and dramatic pauses to heighten the emotional weight of the passage.
3. When you are ready, read it to your partner.
4. Reflect on your experience with your partner. Were certain emotions easier for you to portray? Were certain emotions more challenging to portray? Were there times when you felt more emotional expression was needed in your telling? Less? If you told it again, what would you try differently?
5. Invite feedback of your choosing, or simply ask for appreciation or affirmation.
6. Switch roles.

Sharing (10–15 minutes)

Ask for one or two volunteers who are willing to read their story to the entire group. Emphasize that this is an opportunity for appreciation rather than critique. In keeping with the ground rules, no feedback should be given except that which is invited. Focus instead on appreciating the story and willingness to share.

Closing (10 minutes)

Ask for feedback about the session. Thank everyone for coming. Extinguish the candle or chalice. Clarify when you will have your next meeting and what the participants should bring or prepare.

Session Seven: Practice: Telling a Story to a Supportive Peer
(approx. 70 minutes)

Before You Meet

Ask participants to prepare one story to tell or read. Depending upon their personal goals, experience, or available time, participants should prepare a story to tell or read as they would present it to a congregation or religious education class. They will be presenting their story to one peer and asking only for the feedback they seek.

Gathering (5 minutes)

Help your group mentally transition and become present in the moment at hand. Light a chalice, light a candle, offer a prayer or reading. Remind each other of the purpose and vision of the group and the ground rules you agreed upon. If you have newcomers to the group, make sure to do introductions again.

Warm-Up (15 minutes)

Start the session by listening to a good story together. Choose a favorite picture book, have an experienced member tell a story to everyone, or play a video or audio recording of a professional teller. Offer the story as an opportunity for appreciation rather than critique and to help get everyone in the mood for practicing their own storytelling. Encourage participants to simply experience the story and allow themselves to be affected by the authentic power of the story.

Telling a Story to a Peer (40 minutes)

Ask the group to divide into pairs. The pair will decide which teller will go first. Inform the pairs when half the time has elapsed. Provide the following instructions to the participants:

1. Before beginning their story, the teller informs the listener what feedback, if any, they would like.
2. The teller shares the story they have prepared without interruption.
3. The listener hears the story without interruption.
4. When the story is complete, the listener thanks the teller for offering the story.

5. Briefly reflect on your experience with your partner. How did you feel the telling went? What surprised you about your experience of telling this story? What did you learn from the experience?
6. The teller states again what feedback, if any, he or she would like. The teller can change his or her mind at this point and request no feedback or different feedback, based on the experience of actually telling the story.
7. The teller and the listener switch roles.

Closing (10 minutes)

Invite participants to share what it was like for them to tell their story to a peer. Ask for feedback about the session as a whole. Identify anything in your process that needs to change. Thank everyone for coming. Extinguish the candle or chalice. Clarify when you will have your next meeting and what the participants should bring or prepare.

Session Eight: Practice: Telling a Story to a Supportive Audience
(Length varies per number of presenters.)

Your group may need to plan multiple practice sessions to give participants adequate time to tell their stories and receive feedback.

Before You Meet

Ask participants to prepare one story to tell or read. Depending on their personal goals, experience, or available time, participants should prepare a story to tell or read as they would present it to a congregation or class. They will be presenting their story to the full group and asking only for the feedback they seek. If you have a large group, half the presenters can prepare to tell a story in this session; the other half can present in a future session. Alternatively, you can extend the length of this session accordingly.

Gathering (5 minutes)

Help your group mentally transition and become present in the moment at hand. Light a chalice, light a candle, offer a prayer or reading. Remind each other of the purpose and vision of the group and the ground rules you agreed upon. If this is the first time that some participants will be sharing their story with a group, remind everyone to be supportive and resist giving unsolicited advice or feedback. If you have newcomers to the group, make sure to do introductions again.

Warm-Up (10–15 minutes)

Start the session by listening to a good story together. Choose a favorite picture book, have an experienced member tell a story to everyone, or play a video or audio recording of a professional teller. Offer the story as an opportunity for appreciation rather than critique and to help get everyone in the mood for thinking about and practicing storytelling. Encourage participants to simply experience the story and allow themselves to be affected by the authentic power of the story.

Telling a Story to a Supportive Audience (20 minutes per teller)

The group will gather as one audience, similar to the way a congregation would gather. Ask the group to determine the order of tellers for the evening. If you are stretching these practice tellings over multiple sessions, plan the order the week before.

Provide the following instructions to participants:

1. Before beginning the story, the teller informs the audience what feedback, if any, they would like.
2. The teller shares the story they have prepared without interruption.
3. The audience listens to the story without interruption, although appropriate audience participation is welcome.
4. When the story is complete, the audience thanks the teller for the gift of the story, without critique.

5. Allow the teller to briefly reflect on their experience of telling their story.
6. The teller states again what feedback, if any, he or she would like. The teller can change their mind at this point and request no feedback or different feedback, based on the experience of actually telling the story.

Closing (10 minutes)

Invite participants to share what it was like to tell their story to a supportive audience. Invite participants to share what it was like to be the audience (without offering an unsolicited critique). Ask for feedback about the session as a whole. Identify anything in your process that needs to change. Thank everyone for coming. Extinguish the candle or chalice. If you will be having another meeting, clarify when it will be and what the participants should bring or prepare.

Additional Resources for Storytelling in Worship

Storytelling Collections and Manuals

Conover, Sarah. *Kindness: A Treasury of Buddhist Wisdom for Children and Parents.* Boston: Skinner House, 2001.

> Thirty-two anecdotes and fables from different regions of Asia. Provides source information for each of the stories and sayings.

Conover, Sarah, and Freda Crane. *Ayat Jamilah: Beautiful Signs: A Treasury of Islamic Wisdom for Children and Parents.* Boston: Skinner House, 2004.

> Thirty-nine stories from across the Muslim world. Provides source information for each of the stories and sayings.

Conover, Sarah, and Chen Hui. *Harmony: A Treasury of Chinese Wisdom for Children and Parents.* Boston: Skinner House, 2008.

> Twenty-four stories from China, each with a brief proverb-like version and a more expanded retelling. The preface offers valuable cultural, religious, and philosophical contextualization for the stories. Provides source information for each story.

Edwards, Carolyn McVickar. *The Return of the Light: Twelve Tales from Around the World for the Winter Solstice.* New York: Marlowe, 2000.

> Twelve stories with central themes associated with winter solstice folktales, including "The Theft," "The Surrender," and "The Grace." Each of these global stories includes a valuable introduction about the tale's culture of origin.

Forsyth-Vail, Gail. *Stories in Faith: Exploring Our Unitarian Universalist Principles and Sources Through Wisdom Tales*. Boston: Skinner House, 2007.

> A collection of nineteen wisdom tales adapted from folklore, scripture, history, and biography. While specifically related to Unitarian Universalist Principles and Sources, these stories are suitable for a variety of contexts. Each story includes background and cultural context.

Hewitt, Erika. *Story, Song, and Spirit: Fun and Creative Worship Services for All Ages*. Boston: Skinner House, 2010.

> Nine multigenerational services that weave story and song together into a coherent worship experience. Also includes tips on how to successfully plan and lead multigenerational services.

McDonald, Colleen M. *What If Nobody Forgave? and Other Stories*. 2nd ed. Boston: Skinner House, 2003.

> Nineteen stories organized around the seven Principles of Unitarian Universalism. Each story includes suggestions for telling the stories and questions for reflection.

Moore, Mary Ann. *Hide and Seek with God*. Boston: Skinner House, 1994.

> A series of stories geared toward young children that explore the many different forms and ways that humans know and experience God.

Ross, Jeanette. *Telling Our Tales: Stories and Storytelling for All Ages*. Boston: Skinner House, 1994.

> Thirty-eight tales from a variety of cultures. Each story is accompanied by source and background information, a story outline, and performance suggestions. The book also includes a chapter on telling tales and creating your own stories.

Sawyer, Ruth. *The Way of the Storyteller*. New York: Penguin, 1942.

> The classic guide to storytelling written by one of the most famous storytellers of the twentieth century. Includes a collection of classic tales.

Seal, Dean J. *Church and Stage: Producing Theater for Education, Praxis, Outreach, and Fundraising.* Cambridge, MA: Cowley Publications, 2005.

> A guide to producing theater in congregations, from small bibliodramas performed in worship to full-scale theater productions brought out into the community. Provides advice on recruiting actors, choosing plays, running rehearsals, and marketing shows. Includes two original plays written for churches.

Shedlock, Marie. *The Art of the Story-teller.* Mineola, NY: Dover Publications, 1951.

> The approach and insights to storytelling from one of the most skilled storytellers of the late nineteenth and early twentieth centuries. Originally published in 1915, it includes several classic tales from that era.

Williams, Betsy Hill, ed. *UU & Me!: Collected Stories.* Boston: Skinner House, 2003.

> A brief collection of stories and biographical sketches taken from *UU & Me!,* a Unitarian Universalist magazine for kids.

Picture Books for Adaptation to Storytelling

Alexander, Sue. *Nadia the Willful.* New York: Alfred Knopf, 1983.

> Nadia's older brother Hamed is the only one who can calm her feistiness. When Hamed does not return from the desert, their grief-stricken father forbids anyone to speak his son's name. However, as Nadia longs to speak his name, she grows increasingly surly. A moving tale about keeping our loved ones alive in our hearts.

Andersen, Hans Christian. "The Ugly Duckling," in *I'll Tell You a Story, I'll Sing You a Song: A Parent's Guide to the Fairy Tales, Fables, Songs and Rhymes of Childhood,* retold by Christine Allison. New York: Delacorte Press, 1987.

> A classic for a reason, this tale of the ugly duckling turned beautiful swan speaks of the power of rejection as well as self-transformation and inherent worth.

Bunting, Eve. *Smoky Night*. Orlando, FL: Harcourt Brace, 1994.
   This beautifully illustrated book tells the tale of a young boy who witnesses the shattered glass and flames of the 1992 Los Angeles riots. His mother's calm presence and explanations of what is happening help the boy cope with the confusing, frightening night. When the boy's cat goes missing, finding it turns into an opportunity to build new bridges.

Cooney, Barbara. *Miss Rumphius*. New York: Viking Press, 1982.
   Like her artist grandfather, a young girl vows to go to faraway places and return to live by the sea. Her grandfather tells her she must do one more thing: make the world a more beautiful place. The story touches on themes of work, call, beauty, giving back, art, and having a humble but significant impact on the world.

Cronin, Doreen. *Click, Clack, Moo: Cows That Type*. New York: Simon and Schuster for Young Readers, 2000.
   Farmer Brown's cows find themselves in possession of a typewriter, and all kinds of chaos breaks out among the animals. They demand electric blankets at night, and soon the hens are making demands too. How will labor negotiations work out on Farmer Brown's farm? An amusing story of collective action, labor struggle, the power of education, and the call to grow to our fullest potential.

Fox, Mem. *Wilfrid Gordon McDonald Partridge*. New York: Kane/Miller, 1985.
   Illustrated by Julie Vivas, this is a truly sweet story about a little boy with four names who lives next door to an "old folks home." When he hears that one of the residents has lost her memory, he sets out on a quest to learn from his friends at the home just exactly what a memory is.

Gray, Libba Moore. *Miss Tizzy*. New York: Aladdin, 1993.
   Each day of the week, Miss Tizzy brings fun and surprises to the children on her block. When Miss Tizzy falls ill, the children get the chance to return the favor.

Leaf, Munro. *The Story of Ferdinand*. New York: Viking, 1936.

Ferdinand is a big, ferocious-looking bull whose favorite pastime is smelling flowers. One day, he is accidentally picked for the bullfight. The language is delightfully animated and well suited for telling. A nice vehicle for discussing nonviolence, being oneself, and being kind to animals.

Lewis, Kim. *Floss*. Cambridge, MA: Candlewick Press, 1994.

Floss, a young border collie, is brought to a new farm to learn to herd sheep. Floss works hard to learn herding, but upon seeing the farmer's children playing ball, she forgets about herding sheep. Scolded for playing, Floss works harder to learn to herd. But the children still call to her. The ending and a few other elements are subtly portrayed through beautiful illustrations and need to be adapted for oral telling. It is rich with meaning, however, for young and old.

Lionni, Leo. *Frederick*. New York: Dragonfly Books, 1967.

While the other mice toil to prepare for the upcoming winter, Frederick stores up the beauty of the world. As the gray days of winter go on and the mice's supplies dwindle, they ask Frederick for his stores. Instead of grain, he offers poetry. This story speaks to the place of art in our world of work and productivity.

McLerran, Alice. *The Mountain That Loved a Bird*. New York: Simon and Schuster, 1985.

A tale of a mountain that stood all alone with nothing but the sky to watch until a bird came to rest one day. When the bird must continue its flight, the mountain begs it to stay. Although the bird must go, she promises to return each year. A beautiful story of loneliness, love, and the good that can happen when a heart cracks open.

Munsch, Robert. *Love You Forever*. Toronto: Firefly Books, 2001.

A story of a mother who rocks her son to sleep each night with the song, "I'll Love You Forever, I'll Like You for Always." Each day, even though her son manages to drive her crazy, she sneaks across the bedroom floor to hold him and sing to him, no matter how big he gets and how frustrated she has been. The illustrations offer humor and add to the narrative in ways that could be brought into the telling through adaptation.

Munsch, Robert. *Millicent and the Wind*. Toronto: Annick Press, 1992.
A story about a little girl whose only friend is the wind. She is lonely for another child to play with and asks the wind to help her.

Nygaard, Patricia. *Snake Alley Band*. New York: Doubleday, 1998.
A snake who loves to make shhhh-boom music with his fellow snakes wakes up after hibernating to find they've moved on. Can he learn to make music with creatures other than snakes? A charming tale celebrating diversity that has great potential for bringing the audience into the story as the animal musicians.

Piper, Watty. *The Little Engine That Could: The Complete, Original Edition*. New York: Platt and Munk, 1976.
A retelling of the classic tale that speaks to themes of compassion, equality, and persistence in the face of possible failure.

Sapienza, Marilyn. *Stone Soup*. New York: Newfield Publications, 1996.
A retelling of the classic stone soup story. Two travelers seek to convince an entire village that they can make a delicious soup from nothing but a stone. The villagers are persuaded one by one that the soup would be better with a touch of this and a touch of that. The result is a feast for the whole village, including the hungry travelers. The story is a testimony to the power of community and a nice echo of the loaves and fishes story of the Bible. This version is well suited to telling, although the illustrations are cartoonish. If showing illustrations when reading or telling this story, consider using the version by Jon Muth, described on page 198.

Slobodkina, Esphyr. *Caps for Sale: A Tale of a Peddler, Some Monkeys, and Their Monkey Business*. New York: HarperCollins, 1987.
A peddler winds through town with a tall stack of hats on his head. He stops to sit against a tree and nap. Waking up, he finds monkeys have stolen his caps. He

points his finger at the monkeys and tells them to give him back his hats. They point their fingers in return. He stomps his foot; the monkeys stomp in return. Finally, in disgust, he throws down his own hat and his fortune changes. A fun story with karmic implications.

Stuve-Bodeen, Stephanie. *Elizabeti's Doll.* New York: Lee and Low, 1998.
A very sweet story about a little girl in Tanzania who makes a doll out of rock. Unlike her new infant brother, Elizabeti's doll does not soil her diaper and is too polite to burp. Addresses themes of creativity, imagination, play, nurture, and individuality.

Williams, Karen Lynn. *Circles of Hope.* Grand Rapids, MI: Eerdmans Books for Young Readers, 2005.
The story of a young boy who plants a mango tree as a gift for his infant sister. A goat eats the first seedling, so he replants. Rain on the deforested mountainside washes away his second attempt. Again and again he tries; all the while his mother must take his baby sister to the hospital miles away. A sweet story with gentle suspense. The book is dedicated to Gwen Grant Mellon, whose labor for improved health care in Haiti is a story in itself.

Williams, Vera B. *A Chair for My Mother.* New York: Greenwillow Books, 1982.
Everyone is okay after an apartment catches fire and the neighborhood comes out to help, but Rosa's mother still does not have a comfy chair where she can rest after working on her feet all day. Rosa's family keeps throwing coins in a giant jar, hoping that one day they will be able to buy a chair for her mother.

Woodson, Jacqueline. *The Other Side.* New York: Putnam, 2001.
A story of two little girls, one white and one black, who live on either side of a long fence. "Don't climb over that fence," their mamas tell them. No one told them not to sit on that fence, though.

Yolen, Jane. *Owl Moon*. New York: Philomel, 1987.
> An exquisitely written tale of a young girl who goes owling with her Pa one wintery night. The gripping narrative filled with the earnest wonder of a child makes for a powerful telling.

Picture Books for Reading/Showing

Fox, Mem. *Tough Boris*. Orlando, FL: Harcourt, 1994.
> Boris is tough, like all pirates are tough. Boris is scary, like all pirates are scary. And when his parrot dies, Boris cries, like all pirates cry. An endearing book of few, though powerful, words and engaging illustrations that speak to the universal experience of loss and sadness.

Gray, Libba Moore. *My Mama Had a Dancing Heart*. New York: Orchard Books, 1995.
> Moore presents a beautiful, rhythmic poem that tells of a girl's experience with her mother. From her mother, she learns to celebrate life and its multisensory splendors throughout the seasons. More poem than story, this would work well in place of a reading in a worship service.

Gregory, Valiska. *Looking for Angels*. New York: Simon and Schuster, 1996.
> A little girl wakes up certain that she won't see the angels her grandfather is predicting. As the day progresses, though, she begins to notice the little bits of magic that her grandfather points out. After seeing sunlight lying on the bed, jewels in the garden, and bunnies eating noodles, she is ready to entertain the idea that angels of some sort might just show up. Beautiful watercolor illustrations by Leslie Baker bring to life the beauty of creation and make this story a must-see rather than a must-tell.

Johnson, D. B. *Henry Climbs a Mountain*. Boston: Houghton Mifflin, 2003.
> A bear named Henry, as in Henry David Thoreau, is jailed when he refuses

to pay taxes to a state that would let someone own slaves. His night in jail cannot keep his imagination from flying freely, however. The gentle narrative arc is beautifully written, and the skillful, complex illustrations are engaging. Includes a page summary of Thoreau's actual endeavors. Also see D.B. Johnson's other books in this series: *Henry Builds a Cabin, Henry Hikes to Fitchburg,* and *Henry Works*.

Lionni, Leo. *Swimmy*. New York: Knopf, 1963.
One small fish ventures out to see the marvels of the big ocean for himself, despite the dangers of the bigger creatures around him. He manages to convince a school of small fish just like him that by sticking together, they can do the same.

Martignacco, Carol. *The Everything Seed: A Story of Beginnings*. Berkeley: Tricycle Press, 2006.
The facts of science from the big bang onward are woven into a narrative about the creation of the universe. Poetic language and stunning batik illustrations by Joy Troyer make this a book best suited to hearing and seeing.

Muth, John J. *Stone Soup*. New York: Scholastic Press, 2003.
This version of the classic stone soup folktale tells the story using three Buddhist monks, rather than hungry strangers. Like the more traditional versions, the villagers learn the power of sharing. The incredible artwork of Muth's retelling makes this version an excellent choice if reading the story and showing the illustrations.

Rylant, Cynthia. *The Relatives Came*. New York: Aladdin Paperbacks, 1985.
There is something charming about this story of a carload of relatives that travel through the night from Virginia. It is more poetry than story, yet the text and illustrations speak of appreciation for the comfortably casual but loving closeness of extended family and the kind of communal survival that was commonplace in days gone by.

Seuss, Dr. *Yertle the Turtle and Other Stories*. New York: Random House, 1950.

The wonderful story "Yertle the Turtle" speaks to principles of fairness and equity in society, to hubris and the natural consequences of trying to put oneself above others. It has good narrative structure and could be adapted nicely for telling. "Gertrude McFuzz," another story in the book, is also a wonderful little morality tale. Telling Dr. Seuss is like performing the Shakespeare of children's literature. Because most of Seuss's work is well known, tell it word for word with few mistakes, or the audience will likely be highly distracted. The language's intentional rhythm and rhyme make it challenging to tell without sounding too singsong. If you are an experienced teller who likes a challenge, you'll have fun telling it. This and others works by Dr. Seuss are great to read again and again.

Thomas, Joyce Carol. *Joy*. New York: Hyperion Books for Children, 2001.

This is a beautifully illustrated poem for children. In a few well-chosen words, it uses multisensory seasonal imagery to articulate a mother's love for and appreciation of her child. It is more suitable for use as a reading or recited poem rather than for typical storytelling. Its brevity, word choice, and imagery make it accessible to audiences young and old.